The Straight-Line

The Shortest Distance Between You and Your Results

Bradford F. Spencer, Ph.D.
with Edward L. Monser

ISBN: 9781790381364

I hope

something in this

book helps you to

move forward in your

career!

Ed Morrsel

Acknowledgements

There are so many I owe so much to as I think back on the constructs that have formed this old man's approach and arguably led to the sustaining of my youthful vigor and passion in the field, and in my approach to life in general. And, yes there are many run-on-sentences you will need to put up with. And some of them will end in prepositions...so much for my editor's influence. Oh, I forgot, I did not have an editor for very long. Fired him.

First, I must start with my wife Connie who has put up with many more tense moments than she felt were called for because I was 'a little too frank' at the dinner table with friends. She claims to love me despite my genetic inability to leave the unstated alone, when I feel it will not serve us well. And she is clearly my rock and support system, who is proof that a very capable woman can raise an extremely gifted son while her husband is out of town with clients.

Next on the list: my partners and associates both past and present. The fact is, for good or bad, firms both large and small take on characteristics of the founders. They have had to live and refine this philosophy to integrate what works for them in maximizing effectiveness with their client systems. I cannot help but mention a few by name: Tom Shenk, Hedges Capers, Jr., Susan Peirce, Dan Collett, Stephanie Tran, Shaun Dyke, Tom Coble and Lynn Moore.

And of course, my clients who I have learned so much from and owe a debt that may never be repaid...they are too numerous to name. They extend over many years and include Jim Kerrigan, John Rehfeld, Bob Bateman, Art Coviello, Amit Yoran, Grant Geyer, Richard Patton, John Connors, Bob Brennan, Tony Rose, Jay Coughlan, Claude Ravier, LDS, Corey Thomas, Howard Phanstiel, and of course, the unnamed CFO who appears in Chapter 1.

This work would not be complete without recognizing some of my many mentors who took me under their wings and pushed me to fly: Hedges Capers,

Ph.D., David McClelland, Ph.D., Taibi Kahler, Ph.D., Richard Hill, Harold Long, Ph.D., and Ann Salerno. Their models, and more importantly their modeling of integrity and tough love, has molded my approaches in my personal and business world.

Any errors and obfuscations are mine alone, but I would indeed be remiss not to thank Andrea Schlaerth, Ph.D. for her initial help in wrestling the manuscript into a readable format. To Bret Morris for his patient reading and suggestions, as well as Julia Renedo, Ph.D. and Edward Atienza, M.A. for getting it over the finish line.

And of course, the generous time and contributions of my co-conspirator, Ed Monser. I decided the world did not need another book by a consultant without some hard knock comments by a successful individual who had put the concepts into practice. His straight forward and vulnerable examples recounting the issues he has faced make the work come alive and create a richness and credibility I could not achieve on my own. Being the COO of a $20+ billion company in the midst of acquisitions and divestitures (while creating a dream Corvette) he has proven responsive and resourceful. A great partner.

Thank you all!!!

Bradford F. Spencer, Ph.D.

Table of Contents

Foreword

Sometimes, even a coach needs a coach. I began working with Brad Spencer almost a decade ago when I was the head football coach at Syracuse University, and I continue to rely on his wisdom today in my position as a head coach in the NFL.

Syracuse (my beloved alma mater) was my first head coaching job, and at first, it was overwhelming. I was hired to turn around a once proud football program that had not seen success in many years. To make this happen, I needed to communicate effectively, not just with the players and coaches, but also with the press, the administration, the professors, the alumni, and the fans. This was new to me and I struggled.

I read every leadership book that I could get my hands on, but nothing helped me in the practical way that I needed. So, I reached out to another Syracuse alum whom I knew had taken over a failing company and completely rehabilitated it. I asked him for his best advice, and he said, "You need to call my coach, Brad Spencer."

At the time, I had no idea what he was talking about. I had never heard of an "executive coach" or a "leadership coach" or whatever the correct term is. And I was stunned that my business tycoon friend had ever needed a "coach."

To say I was skeptical would be an understatement, but I boarded a plane to Los Angeles a few weeks later to meet with Brad Spencer. And it was, without a doubt one of the best decisions I have ever made.

To my great relief, Brad was not a stuffy intellectual full of psycho-babble. He was completely no-nonsense. He didn't ask for blind trust, he showed me that his leadership approach is data driven, and I am a guy that really likes data. That trip marked the beginning of a professional relationship and friendship that changed the way I lead.

Brad taught me to communicate more effectively. He taught me to pay attention to and understand what motivates different individuals. I think the most important lesson that I've learned from Brad, however, is how to take a hard look at myself. I know what I am really good at, and now I also know what I am not very good at; and this self-awareness has been a game-changer. As an example, when I began working with Brad, I thought I was a straight-forward communicator. I soon learned that what was well thought-out and made perfect sense in my head did not always come out of my mouth. Dr. Spencer uses Straight-Line communication, and he taught me to use Straight-Line communication. Now I don't wonder if I've gotten my message across, I know that I've gotten my message across. (And understanding my starting point, I have to wonder if Chapter 3, *"What it Ain't,"* was written solely for me?)

Dr. Spencer's approach to problems is brilliant and very often irreverent. He is a humble expert in leadership, executive development, and management with over forty years of experience with a wide range of clients from Fortune 100 CEO's to Silicon Valley start-ups. Brad's book, *The Straight-Line* is as direct and no-nonsense as he is. It is full of practical approaches and principals that I use every day. The strikingly vulnerable examples provided by Ed Monser help bring the concepts to life for those in corporate America.

Leadership itself is an on-going process that needs continual revision and adaptation to the changing landscape of an organization's needs. I consistently use my resources to seek the best experts I can find for guidance, given any current set of circumstances. *The Straight-Line* is now at the top of my list.

The Straight-Line will undoubtedly transform how you communicate in your professional and personal lives and all will have won for it.

Doug Marrone, Head Coach
Jacksonville Jaguars
September 2018

Chapter 1

A Wake-up Call

"More faults are often committed while we are trying to oblige than while we are giving offence."

-TACITUS

When I answered the 6:00 a.m. wake-up call, I felt as if I had just fallen asleep. Late the night before, my flight from Los Angeles had landed in New York City. By the time I made it to the hotel room, it was 1:30 a.m.

Slightly later that morning, I arrived at the Plaza Hotel's Palm Court restaurant—at the time, one of downtown Manhattan's primary "power breakfast" destinations. I was a few minutes early for my 7:00 a.m. breakfast meeting with Jeff, a newly minted CFO for a rapidly growing four-hundred-million-dollar holding company. Dressed in my best uniform, a dark suit with crisp white shirt and tie, I was still somewhat bleary eyed and definitely sleep deprived.

I entered the iconic restaurant where Jeff was already seated and ready for his second cup of coffee. On the table in front of him lay his carefully crafted agenda. It was our first meeting. Once I sat down, we immediately plunged into business. After my third yawn, he looked directly at me.

"You seem really tired," he said.

"I'm exhausted. I'm still on Pacific Standard Time, so it's 4:10 in the morning for me," I said as I took a gulp of tepid coffee.

The Straight-Line

I added I had had a busy week leading up to the flight. Once I had arrived in the city the night before, I had gone to dinner and had drinks with a client. The event had ended well past my typical bedtime. Having done the cross-country plane commute countless times before, my time zone fatigue felt completely familiar.

"Perhaps we should reschedule," Jeff said. **"After all, I'm not paying for advice from an exhausted consultant."**

His words are forever burned in my memory. They scared the life out of me. Jeff was not angry or upset—only slightly frustrated that he had prepared for a meeting he now felt needed rescheduling. My initial response was to reassure him I was ready. Instead, I acknowledged I might not be in top form today. In the end, I was petrified I had fallen short of his expectations; I felt he had correctly questioned my competence, and I feared I had just lost a client.

Meanwhile, he had already buried his words in the past and held no residual resentment. After the initial discomfort I experienced during our brief exchange, we spent the next half hour engaging in pleasant conversation. At the same time, we didn't address the agenda items. Instead, we postponed any substantive discussion for the next day.

Up to that point in my career, all my clients would have continued the meeting without questioning my ability to be optimally productive. They might have been completely unsatisfied and asked themselves, "Am I paying this guy to yawn three times in ten minutes?" But they would have said nothing, which would have resulted in a far less effective meeting than otherwise possible.

Jeff's insistence to reschedule underscores the premise of this book. By leaving himself slightly vulnerable and stating he didn't want an exhausted consultant, he was also telling me what he did want: a committed professional ready to tackle the task at hand with alacrity. What he said demonstrates Straight-Line communication.

What Straight-line Communication Is *Not*

When I've described my first meeting with Jeff to others, the response is typically, "How could he be so insensitive?" But I've come to realize Jeff was anything but insensitive. Furthermore, my initial shock regarding what he said was a conditioned response—one with origins many of us share.

Back when we were little kids, many of us were reprimanded for innocently stating the obvious. For example, we might have said, "Mommy, you look fat," or asked, "Daddy, why don't you have your seatbelt on?"

Sayings such as, "If you can't say anything nice, don't say anything at all," reflect our culture's emphasis on **avoidant communication**, which is a person's unwillingness to raise a topic because he or she:

1. Fears it may leave him or her vulnerable.
2. Believes it may be too sensitive.
3. Thinks someone's feelings may be hurt, including their own.
4. May be ejected or rejected from a group.

Ejection and rejection, in particular, are primal fears with evolutionary origins tracing back to our hunter-and-gatherer past—a prehistoric time when our survival depended on group membership. Furthermore, being rejected by the opposite sex would have thwarted our ability to pass along our genes and perpetuate our bloodlines.

What Straight-line Communication *Is*

Avoidant communication's opposite is Straight-Line communication, which is *being open to the point of vulnerability by expressing our honest and complete reaction to what is occurring. The objective of Straight-Line communication is to leave individuals and organizations more productive and guided toward reaching their goals.*

Society's Mixed Messages about Straight-line Communication

We'll explore the differences between avoidant and Straight-Line communication later in this book. For now, consider how this dichotomy appears in our everyday language.

On the one hand, "ignorance is bliss" generally has positive overtones. On the other hand, "don't rock the boat" is decidedly negative. Our parents may have told us the topics appropriate for polite conversation (i.e. weather, sports, and music) and subjects that should be avoided at all cost (e.g. politics, sex, and religion). The bottom line is, from a young age, we quickly learned that, when in doubt, keeping our mouths shut is the best and correct option.

Support for Straight-line Communication

That morning at the Plaza Hotel, Jeff's Straight-Line communication expressed to me what he was experiencing as we sat together. In his judgment, my fatigue undermined my ability to provide him the precise support he needed. He was right: "When we're exhausted, none of us is as sharp and alert as we could be." Jeff had the integrity and courage to reveal what was on his mind.

According to his boss—the company's CEO, who recommended Jeff contact me—I was the best-qualified person to help Jeff face the specific challenge before him. Meanwhile, Jeff was charged to solve big problems, and he was under tremendous pressure to deliver remarkable results. His honesty had a profound and lasting impact on my behavior.

In addition, Jeff appreciated how I responded to his dissatisfaction when he said, "After all, I'm not paying for advice from an exhausted consultant." Had I objected with "No, I'm okay; why don't we continue as scheduled" or any number of other defensive postures intended to protect my wounded ego, I'm certain our relationship would have ended at The Plaza. Instead, we met the next day, and we've continued to work together for twenty more years. As

Jeff's example illustrates, Straight-Line communication is an unparalleled way to express our candid perspective. When properly deployed in business, it is a breakthrough approach for the global age.

Today, competitors in industry are unfettered by political boundaries, and information is exchanged around the world as soon as it's produced. As a result, organizations have less time than ever to make high-quality decisions. Thus, the challenge faced is clear: under present-day pressures, how do individuals and organizations increase effective communication, which leads to positive action, while minimizing the bottlenecks and destructive forces of poor communication? In the following chapters, we put forth an answer to this question will be revealed. Further insight will be gained into what Straight-Line communication is, what it isn't, and how it has dramatically improved the performance of highly motivated professionals in every business setting.

The Straight-Line

Ed Monser's Practical Input:

What Corporate Wants to Hear

It is fascinating how many shades of gray exist around someone's ability to use Straight-Line communication (both with others and themselves). The ability and courage to say the things that need to be said, and to break down the barriers that slow progress, is special and absolutely required for someone to be a leader. People that avoid saying things out of fear or are trying to avoid conflict or confrontation cannot be effective in a fast-moving business environment. And very importantly, if employees are going to follow someone, they need to believe that person is worthy of their trust. Followers must always know where they stand with their leader. The ability to generate trust comes from the effort of using Straight-Line communication. Candor in both directions removes barriers, and when there are few barriers, an organization moves forward with speed and efficiency.

When our company is selecting leaders for new positions, we have an annual, disciplined Organization Review process led by our CEO. In that process we can review up to fifteen hundred people. This is a formal process where issues and opportunities are aggressively discussed and debated. After the reviews are completed each of the people's picture, work history, performance, and potential are posted in our Development Room to make it easy to see and understand who can do what for the company. We are constantly combing through this data for people who exhibit four specific special qualities.

We look for individuals who are strategic thinkers and are forward-thinking. They understand from what direction we have come and in what direction we need to move in today's ever-changing business environment.

We seek out those with a knack for inspiration—the type of hardy, dynamic person, who can communicate the future in a way that encourages people to sign on and work hard for the duration of a project or program.

Needless to say, we look for competency. A deep understanding of the critical issues, technologies, and relationships indicates the ability to achieve positive results. People that can and do get things done is essential. We look for collaboration skills and the ability to build effective teams and structures, essential to solving the needs of our customers in a dynamic world.

Lastly, we look for honesty and straightforward communications. Candor, caring, and constancy in dealing with people are all indications of an authentic person who generates trust.

We believe you have to have all of these qualities to be effective. As we evaluate candidates, we often find people who are excellent at strategic thinking, hardiness, and competency; honesty and direct communications, however, generate the largest variation. We have weighted this trait accordingly, and on more than one occasion, this is the one that tips the scales for who is selected and who is not selected.

"Jennifer" was being groomed for many years to have a large President role in the organization—the position would run an entire platform of multiple divisions with billions of dollars in revenues, essentially a very high-level job.

Jennifer was technically excellent in a very dynamic industry; her competency was extraordinary. She had a deep knowledge of the market, and her strategic plans and projections were always insightful and impactful. Her relationships with customers were very positive, and her team agreed she inspired them to do their best work. She had been systematically promoted through the ranks and was the obvious choice to take over for the incumbent.

But something was missing. As she was stepping up to this higher level and was no longer just reporting down but also reporting up to corporate, we found that she had a problem making commitments she could not keep. In the beginning, these commitments would be small, relatively insignificant things. For instance, she would say whatever she needed to say to get out of the meeting and evade debate. Then she began saying whatever she thought corporate wanted to hear without any real intention of acting on it. Then it became clear that she was telling corporate one thing and then reversing her position and telling her management teams the opposite. She was on a slippery slope, trying to play both sides, to win the hearts of everyone at the cost of her own honesty and integrity. I am certain that in her own mind she had rationalized her dishonesty because her division had a history of doing very well and generated consistent profits. Unfortunately, things were starting to unwind as some key market shifts were underway and her group was not investing in the technology needed to lead the market or even to defend itself. The discussions needed to initiate the needed investments were being avoided with corporate and the seeds of market share loss were being sown.

As this behavior became more and more obvious, the doubts from the senior executives grew proportionally. We could not get an honest commitment from her. It was frustrating to think we had over two decades of investment in this person! But she couldn't change. she finally had to leave the corporation. Her division may have been doing well now, but a lack of Straight-line communication corrodes relationships over time. Decreased efficiency, market position and profitability were inevitable with this kind of behavior.

We needed a new leader and ended up looking towards an entirely different business platform. We found "Kate," who consistently used Straight-Line communication. Kate was exceptionally talented and was incredibly comfortable asking for help, challenging ideas, and admitting when she needed more information or more time to solve a problem. Unfortunately, she didn't have all the specialized technical background, didn't know all the customers, and didn't know the market and its attendant sensitivities of growth and profitability. Jennifer had all those qualities, but she lacked Straight-Line communication skills. Kate was honest and straight forward. This trumped all those other deficiencies. We would make the investment in her to learn, but we would not compromise on Straight-Line communication. Kate got the job.

Under Kate's leadership we got a complete transformation of the business. The changes and challenges of the evolving market were put on the table and open, Straight-Line communications exposed the need for a number of new investments. The market segmentation was changing and a family of new products were needed to support this change. With Kate's leadership, we were able to deliver the new technology and products faster than ever for this business, and were able to fight effectively for our share of the market.

It is awfully sad to watch someone rationalize his or her dishonesty. It is understandable to want to perform well and achieve goals, but it can never come at the cost of trust. Straight-Line communication has always been the defining issue in the vetting process for promotions I have overseen. We never compromise on that. The risk is too high to act otherwise.

The Straight-Line

Chapter 2

Straight and Speed

"Sometimes you have to look reality in the eye and deny
it."

-Garrison Keeler

Straight Talk

When I first opened my practice, I took on several "full time/part time" roles for clients. At the time I was newly married with a very healthy mortgage payment and could ill afford to lose these clients as this was the back bone of my security. In essence I was a hired gun to fill a role paid as a 1099 rather than a W2. As you all know, one of the reasons to hire 1099 employees is they are very easy to terminate for any reason.

One of my early assignments had me acting in a product management role reporting to a very bright VP of marketing. I will call her Barbara (as with all the people I discuss in the book her name has been changed to protect the innocent.) As a VP, she was responsible for overseeing the development of a product from inception to packaging and pricing. She had climbed the corporate ranks through a series of product hits, hard work, and intimidation. Regarding the last point, most of us had come to both respect her natural ability and fear her.

Rather than regret her reputation, she seemed to wear it as if it were a badge of honor. She had no qualms about publicly berating dissenters during meetings both big and small. On several occasions, she had fired those who had directly reported to her when they had disagreed with her decisions. And

11

if she disapproved of an employee who wasn't a direct report, then that poor soul would be guaranteed a very tough time in meetings she attended.

During meetings she'd run, participants were both in awe of her business mind and terrified of being scorned in front of their peers. I recall one such meeting where Barbara was describing a new product-line extension that would make a superb addition to an already popular brand.

She described a brilliant roll out. Her pitch reflected her characteristic charisma and quick wit. Upon launch, the product would fly off shelves, and because of its positioning, it would keep the velocity of sales for its companion products jumping off the shelf.

"This will compete in the premium segment, which explains the high price point I've attached to it," she said.

Most of us were astonished. The product had no premium attributes, and the line in which it was positioned was not high end either. Meanwhile, everyone in the conference room, including me, smiled and nodded. Our nonverbal expressions reflected an endorsement of her pricing strategy.

But once the meeting concluded and Barbara was nowhere in sight, it's as if all of us collectively freed our held tongues and stated our true opinions: *What was she thinking? There's no way this will help the brand. I'm so glad I'm not the only one who thought her plan was crazy,* and more.

Although the flurry of post-meeting dissent signaled disagreement, no one had spoken up during the meeting itself. I wouldn't characterize our silence as lying—unless you define withholding one's opinion a fib. At the same time, Barbara interpreted the nodding heads and smiles as our approval of her plan, and she moved forward with it.

Just as we had feared, upon launch, the product failed to come close to the sales projections. It wasn't a complete flop, but it would definitely not make it on Barbara's greatest hits list. For fourteen months, the product, with its overly ambitious price tag, languished. Worse yet, it was not the next great item in the line to keep the robust sales moving.

The reality is that none of us practiced Straight-Line communications. If we had done so the time to rectify the situation would have probably been much shorter and the organizations top and bottom line would have benefitted.

To her credit, Barbara eventually realized her mistake. She reduced the price and reintroduced it. Armed with its lowered cost, it soon met the ambitious sales and revenue projections of her original plan.

We'll explore next why scenarios similar to what I described play out—in varying degrees of severity—in conference rooms across the country.

Avoidant Communication

As a consultant, I regularly attend meetings throughout the United States. Typically, my role is to observe what takes place during meetings in order to identify and address an organization's problems. In conference room after conference room, I witness what I experienced twenty-five years ago working with Barbara: avoidant communication.

Previously, we defined *avoidant communication* as people's unwillingness to raise a topic because they fear it may leave them vulnerable, it may be too sensitive, someone's feelings may be hurt, including possibly their own, or they may be ejected or rejected from a group. Simply put, avoiding communication is an unwillingness to raise a topic where the results may be painful. Interestingly, one may not even be conscious of the fact driving their behavior: fear.

A commonly agreed-upon principle in psychology, which has precious few such universal agreements, is humans seek pleasure and avoid pain. We humans do define *pain* differently, however. Examples are idiosyncratic and

13

highly dependent on distinct personality types, but may be identified by one or more of the following causes of pain in an interpersonal business communication setting:

- Hurting someone's feelings
- Being rejected
- Not being viewed as a team player
- Losing a client
- Physical harm
- Losing status or prestige or both
- Not being successful
- Losing a position
- Disappointing others
- Losing a friend

Silence and Avoidant Communication

I find the majority of problems with avoidant behavior come from not speaking up, as opposed to politically-oriented comments made to curry favor or please others. In fact, I believe in an overwhelming number of cases, the transgression is a sin of omission rather than commission. Regardless, the results are often the same.

When we're afraid, silence is what occurs in the majority of cases. When people aren't speaking up, often it's a result of disagreement. To avoid speaking up is not the same as lying to a person in these cases, but the result is the same.

In reference to the events I described at the beginning of the chapter, no one erred by saying, "Barbara that's a great idea!" In other words, people who aren't feeling safe don't necessarily lie to your face; they are often just quiet. This approach is one of safety, which is identical to our reaction in the wild.

Not that the Barbara example needs to get any more complex, but clearly another phenomenon was occurring—the unexpected surprise of the premium-pricing construct. This was an unexpected change for everyone in the room, and a departure from the group's understanding of the product line's positioning, which had been well thought out.

Speed to Decision-Making

Jack Welch, former CEO and Chairman of the Board of GE, is a bit of an enigma in business lore, and some of his practices now draw criticism and controversy. One question is not debated, however: he knew how to build stockholder value by focusing relentlessly on CORE (those variables that will affect stock price). Of course, that was his job, he did it very well, and his stockholders will gladly attest to that fact. In his bestselling book on business philosophy, *Winning*, he includes a short chapter on what he labels the "biggest little dirty secret in business." Chapter 2 is only 10 pages long, but it is the sole reason one of my clients bought 310 copies to have his managers read. It is entitled CANDOR.

This particular chapter bemoans the lack of candor in business environments, and documents Welch's quest to change that at GE, particularly around the debates concerning the CORE. CORE activities of a business are defined as those functions that if they dramatically improve or flounder will affect the stock price one way or the other. All other functions are referred to as CONTEXT. Your role as CEO is to focus your limited time and energy on CORE. Of the three major reasons Welch lists why candor pays off, there is one specific reason I find extremely compelling: it "generates speed."

While Mr. Welch is great at building value, he is very far from being a psychologist. He does refer to a professor of philosophy for an explanation of why people avoid candor. He, in turn, references an 18th century German philosopher, Immanuel Kant. The explanation for "why" boils down to: "it is just easier to not be STRAIGHT." While that is accurate, that is not the causation for the lack of candor in most of us.

The real reason is fear. And what are we afraid of? That is actually initially dependent on your personality type, but the shorthand version is fear of one or more results: rejection by another person, ejection from the group whose norms you have just violated, or of being viewed as not a team player, among others. But in essence, it is always a *LOSS* we fear.

The Process of Change in the Brain

A very simplistic way to look at the brain (please check with your local neurologist) is that three lobes are involved when change occurs. Whenever a change takes place, it is first processed in the lobe of brain called the amygdala. The amygdala is also where the pain avoidance mechanism takes place. From an evolutionary standpoint, the amygdala is one of the brain's more primitive parts. It resides in the cerebrum's medial temporal lobe. We share the amygdala with reptiles—our distant evolutionary relatives who have roamed the earth far longer than we have. Because the amygdala traces back to them, it is also called the reptilian brain.

For both reptiles and humans, the amygdala has provided the fight-or-flight mechanism. It has given us the ability to learn the skills required to hunt food and avoid being prey. As far as reptiles are concerned, based on the hundreds of millions of years they've roamed the earth, the amygdala has served them well. It is the sole enabling reason they have been able to survive. The amygdala is the only lobe reptiles have. Meanwhile, humans have evolved more sophisticated lobes.

In reference to my meeting at the consumer products company, we first processed Barbara's surprise announcement regarding her plans in the amygdala. And the result was our survival mechanism kicked in. While we were not conscious of it, our ability to process complex thoughts was shut down. Think about it: a lizard is not capable of complex thinking as humans define the term. Fortunately, most of the fears that occur in the amygdala never come to reality.

Fear of survival was not the major issue in the room. Yet we sought to avoid the pain associated with a fear we were not conscious of at that moment. This scenario in a business setting is all too common. If someone had cautiously questioned the pricing of the product, we may have had a great success story, or we could have revisited the question much sooner. As a result, the corporation would have made its projections with all the associated trickle-down effects of greater profitability.

Our Reptilian Brain—Fear Rules Our Decisions

Ann Salerno, co-founder of CCMC Inc., an international training and development company, created a model known as the Change Cycle. It is a groundbreaking management model that explains how the reptilian brain stem, mammalian brain, and human brain, together influence our decision-making when we're confronted with change. She describes how the amygdala acts predictably and always in the same fashion.

Throughout human history, the amygdala has caused us to respond to change as a potential danger. Thus, our initial response is fear-driven. This results in finding the quickest route to safety when confronted with danger, which has allowed us as a species to make it through life-threatening situations. Those who survived have passed their genes to subsequent generations.

In modern life, however, most of our decisions do not have life-or-death consequences. But despite moving from the bushes to the boardroom, we still find ourselves relying on our reptilian brains. Unfortunately, neglecting to replace lower-level amygdala-based decision making with higher-level brain functions often leads to unfavorable outcomes and, in particular, not being straightforward in our communication.

When the change is consciously raised, you have a much higher probability to move action to a different part of your brain, to cognitively process the question at hand. As a result, you are much more likely to have a balanced and logical response. But your response needs to be conscious, and it is generally accepted that 95 percent of our responses are made on automatic pilot.

The bottom line is simple: unless you are able to move beyond the reptilian brain, fear will dominate your decision-making process. Thus, in the product meeting, the potential benefits of speaking up did not receive the appropriate weight. When the reptilian brain is processing the information, it is only concerned about the basic survival question. Thus, the positive potential is not in the equation. In order to consider the potential upsides, you must move out of the reptilian brain complex – cognitively.

Our Mammalian Brain—Complex Thinking

The next lobe of the brain discussed in Ann Salerno's book, *The Change Cycle: How People Can Survive and Thrive in Organizational Change* (Berrett-Koehler, 2008), is the *mammalian brain.* As its name indicates, it's a lobe found in mammals but not in reptiles. Mammals are capable of activities that require much more complex thinking ability than reptiles. As an example, wolves can hunt in packs and collaborate to obtain food. This is far beyond the abilities of any reptile

The Human Brain—Consciously Taking Control

But while a horse probably can tell the difference between two and ten bales of hay, a mammal needs what is called the *complex brain* (or *human brain)* to figure out how to make a financial ledger to account for the hay itself. This advanced thinking takes place in an entirely different lobe of the brain, called the frontal cortex, which doubled or tripled in size in primates approximately two to three million years ago. In regard to the meeting with Barbara, we needed to be in this part of our brain to understand and comment intelligently on the pricing question when it arose.

So, it is possible to explain why we are not straightforward with each other from a biological standpoint. The vast majority, if not all, of business decisions require the complex brain. The question is: how do we develop the ability to be in the correct part of the brain for the function needed?

I find this to be a recurring issue when I explore topics with senior executives. I'm somewhat famous for asking, "What went into your decision formula?" They don't need very long to recognize the only variable they were weighing were the downside risks—in other words, the potential losses. This is the first clue they were stuck in the reptilian brain while attempting to make decisions far beyond the capabilities or purpose of that lobe.

To understand and see how pervasive this sense of loss can be on decisions, let's look at the work of William Bridges, consultant and author of *Managing Transitions: Making the Most of Change* (Perseus Books, 2009). He identified seven distinct buckets losses fall into:

1. Loss of control
2. Loss of turf
3. Loss of meaning
4. Loss of attachments
5. Loss of structure
6. Loss of future
7. Loss of identity

When we're confronted with change, we first consider what loss we might experience. In this light, we can see why so many decisions are designed not to optimize, but rather, to minimize the downside. When we responded to Barbara's presentation, we were not lying to her; we just were not driving with all eight cylinders engaged.

We were not consciously aware one or more of these losses were paralyzing us. Rather, like an airplane on autopilot, we allowed our reptilian brain to drive our decisions. While *we may have believed* we were consciously evading speaking out, the reality is avoiding expressing what was on our minds occurred on a subconscious level. In fact, research indicates 95 percent of our behavior patterns are subconscious.

Establishing the Right Responses

The approaches and the methods we use to deal with issues are thus similar to well-worn paths. On a college campus, you will find sidewalks, and then you will find the worn paths indicating what students actually take to walk to class. Similarly, we each have our own mental shortcuts.

The same is true for processing information. We humans develop our preprogrammed paths over time and with repetition. We are almost totally unaware we are using them when we are doing so. For example, when a person approaches issues through his or her feelings versus thinking, this is an unconscious response that has major ramifications on how the information is handled.

When we become conscious and mentally review (or better yet, compose a list of) the potential positive outcomes, they will often offset any losses. This had better be the case, because the source of the fear is often rational and based on experience. The truth is, fear is sometimes justified.

When you think through fear and understand it comes from the processing of the frontal cortex, the fear of loss is often justified. If avoidant communication has kept you employed and you've relied on it to close deals, taking on a new communication strategy may seem unnecessary, if not downright dangerous. On the other hand, if you maintain the status quo and refuse to consider the consequences of avoidant communication, you may eventually find yourself unemployed or with slumping sales without any mechanism to improve future outcomes. In hindsight, when you consider the sales people you trust most, they've probably earned your respect because they provided an objective opinion, even if it didn't serve their bottom-line interests.

In 2002, Dr. Daniel Kahneman won the Nobel Prize in economics. His best-selling book, *Thinking, Fast and Slow* (Farrar, Straus and Giroux, 2011), describes how humans seek to avoid a loss when there is more perceived risk than potential gain. He identified how messages of potential loss affect parts of the brain wired for disgust and pain. His research demonstrates how the brain impacts decisions such as whether you will purchase a product or not. This aligns with the avoidant communication message.

If the change is consciously raised, you are much more likely to move to a different part of your brain to process the question at hand. Furthermore, you are also much more likely to have a balanced and logical response: but it needs to be conscious.

The bottom line is simple: unless you are able to move beyond the reptilian brain, fear will dominate your decision-making process. When the reptilian brain is processing the information, it is only concerned about the basic survival question. Thus, the positive potential is not in the equation. In order to consider the potential upsides, you must move out of the reptilian brain complex.

Effectively using Straight-Line communication, which requires our human brain, takes effort and is not easy: but is clearly beneficial. Often the lesson of taking a path of least resistance is to avoid it altogether. The quality of your decisions will prove the effort you make is worth it by a considerable margin.

The Straight-Line

Ed Monser's Practical Input:

Results of changing to Straight-Line Communication

The satisfaction I had upon being promoted to division president was short-lived. The transition was set for that September, just one month after our yearly budgets were set in place. At our financial review meeting, the outgoing president presented the coming year's budgetary goals and then handed off ownership to me. The pressure of my new position as division president was amplified: not only did I want to live up to the expectations of my new superiors, but now I felt an increased responsibility for those under my leadership whose bonuses were tied to a budget. I had assumed the responsibility, and now this budget and set of goals were mine. It was clear that if we did not hit our financial goals, my team would not get paid, and I felt that they would point the finger of blame at me.

I quickly set about to understand the goals I had been tasked with achieving. Of the three-hundred-million-dollar annual budget, two-thirds came from repeat business. These were solid, predictable accounts with little probability of significant change. The remaining third, however, was attributed to new business, accounts that we had not yet won. In trying to understand the figures better, I went to our sales teams and asked them to show me the projects they expected to win. By their accounting, there were only five to eight million-dollar accounts in the new projects queue—and even if we did win all fifteen accounts we were chasing that totaled eighty-five million dollars, we would still be fifteen million dollars short. On top of this, their "hit rate" (their success in actually winning an account they bid on) was averaging one out of every three. In other words, the eighty-five million dollars was really only thirty million dollars, far short of our one-hundred-million-dollar goal. I was instantly uncomfortable with the facts, and the sales managers' silence did nothing to reassure my anxiety. No one was talking about the glaring discrepancy right underneath our noses.

I needed more information. Believing this was not a problem restricted to sales in my division, but rather a problem with deeper roots in the way projects were managed, I selected a group of our company's top project salespersons from around the world to meet in Minneapolis. My goal was to find out what we needed to do to perform better.

In calling the meeting to order, I explained my reason for dragging these managers away from their busy offices: our system was deeply flawed. We needed to change. Again, as with my division sales managers, the room was silent. Finally, I admitted to the group that I was nervous, maybe even fearful, about how things would turn out for my team, for the company, and of course, for my own future if we did not address this problem. Using Straight-Line communication with the group about my fear of losing shifted the atmosphere of the meeting. After another uncomfortably long period of time, I heard a tentative voice in the back of the room say, "Do you really want to know?" As soon as this individual spoke up, the room relaxed. People realized this brave person would not be denounced for speaking honestly; soon others began chiming in with their ideas. Before long, the discussion brought up myriad issues, all of them rooted in a systemic inability to use Straight-Line communication.

There were many critical issues. Internal competition, lack of shared data, inappropriately scaled metrics, redundant technologies, absence of a system to attribute credit/reward, and a disconnect between upper management and the language of project pursuits. Other issues, not as critical, surfaced as well. Lack of cultural awareness between multi-national projects, a weak system of accountability, inadequate leadership training—the list became quite long.

As people contributed ideas to the ways in which we could improve, I was struck with how much time and energy had been dedicated to evading the solutions that seemed so obvious to the group before me. Fear had clamped mouths shut. I pondered the question: how could the environment be changed to eliminate fear and encourage Straight-Line communication like these at all times? We needed a new system of communication that would dramatically improve the speed of decisions in pursuing projects; we needed this speed so we could win!

Over the next year, we put in place new strategies for project management and new metrics for success that not only addressed the problem areas, but also built trust and encouraged Straight-Line communication. Over time, we built an environment where people could safely make promises—and reliably deliver on them. One year later, we had moved our pursued projects queue of eighty-five million dollars (with only a one-third hit rate) to one of six hundred million dollars; a couple of years after that, it was closer to three billion dollars. The end result of our newfound systemic policy of Straight-Line communication: a much bigger universe to participate in...and much bigger profits.

In looking back, it is fun to also realize that six of the attendees at that first meeting in Minneapolis have become life-long friends and companions on numerous adventures. We all are retired or nearing retirement, and it is a real treasure to have a group like this where Straight-Line communication remains the norm! The adventure continues.

Chapter 3

What It Ain't

"Ye shall know the truth, and the truth shall make you mad."

-Aldous Huxley

"I just can't take one more QBR!!"

This was the opening salvo of a call from Peter, an extremely effective president of the largest divisions of a hugely successful $20 billion-plus corporation. He was going to resign! The QBRs (quarterly business reviews) were rough, but I thought he enjoyed the tough challenges.

The Bully at the Pulpit

The CEO and chairman of the board, known for his brutal honesty and penetrating manner designed to get at the truth, had just berated him in the QBR. While I did not work directly with this CEO, I had come to respect this no-nonsense approach from a distance. It turns out, he was on the warpath about cost overruns in software program implementation and had taken his frustration out on Peter. When I told Peter not to personalize it, his response was telling, "It is awfully hard not to personalize it when he calls you an a—hole."

I listened in amazement as the diatribe unwound and couldn't help but recognize that the qualities I had been admiring in this CEO were certainly absent from this meeting. His anger was not about using Straight-Line communication at all; rather, he was being a bully from an unassailable pulpit, taking his rage out on a person with no defenses.

As Peter recounted the dialogue, it was clear that the CEO's ranting had nothing to do with helping the organization or the individual improve. It demonstrated no willingness to be vulnerable. This is NOT using Straight-Line communication.

Let me make it clear: this is not a book condoning a return to autocratic management or rudeness. That style does not work in the long run. The collaborative training for effective managers and executives in the economic boom following WWII caught on precisely because the evidence showed overwhelmingly that the new approaches led to higher productivity. As for any system or management style, if it does not improve output over time, it will not (and should not) be adopted.

In his fascinating book, *The Big Short: Inside the Doomsday Machine* (W. W. Norton & Company, 2010), Michael Lewis refers to a culture of intimidation created at AIG under the management of Joe Cassano. The vivid, obscenity-laced portrait painted by Lewis indicates that Cassano was nothing short of a bully. I don't know him, and it may not be true (I have read enough of Lewis's work to respect both his research and the fact that he does not waste time on character assassination, which gives credibility to his portrayal), but I have met a dozen like Cassano. Many of you know a bully masquerading as a manager or executive who expects you to agree "OR ELSE." This is not meant to be a book to give sage advice on how (or even to encourage you) to better deal with the Joe Cassanos of your world. Bullies are an extreme example, and there are many books and courses on "how to deal with difficult people."

The threats and rewards are clear, and you must choose to use Straight-Line communication and its potential costs. Having said that, it takes a high degree of courage, or stupidity, to confront a dictator. It was reported by the CIA that when a staff member of Saddam Hussein disagreed with him in a meeting, he took out his pistol and shot the person dead on the spot. You may not be surprised to learn he faced no opposition to his ideas after that little incident.

Some may tell you to look in the mirror to determine if you are using Straight-Line communication and recognize if you invite the same in return. The fact is, friends and employees will tell you they want honest feedback but subtly, and not so subtly, say the opposite. There are many ways this is communicated.

Dealing with Fragile Personalities

So, let's spend a minute on how and why, despite their words, people really don't want Straight-Line communication. One of the more common reasons is fragility. When you drop a fragile vase, it shatters with no hope of putting the pieces back together. Some of your acquaintances and coworkers send out signals they will break if confronted in any negative way. The ramification is that you will be responsible for them feeling badly, possibly becoming depressed, and thus eventually committing suicide—all for giving your honest experience of the moment. And the fact is that your "truth" may not be the real "truth," and you are now a murderer with no justification, other than a stubborn bone to pick that led to the demise of a poor and innocent victim. Your actions based on your belief that there is value in honesty, will have led to such deep hurt that the relationship will never be able to return to a positive one again. Of course, this is merely imaginary, not the reality.

"Victimization" is the key issue here. While not entirely universal, if the vibe you are getting is "poor me": you are dealing with a victim mind-set. You are being asked to rescue this type of person by shielding him or her from your own candor. When the sense you are getting is, "I am hurt so easily that any attempts at confrontation will wound me," you are being set up. Depending on your upbringing, your guilt or shame (they are very different) will come to the aid of the other and leave the elephant in the room unmentioned. This will ultimately prevent a genuine resolution of the problem or intimacy in the relationship.

Forgive one of my digressions, as I distinguish between the Western Judeo-Christian ethic of guilt, and the Eastern Buddhist-Shinto concept of shame. Simply put, when we are experiencing guilt, we are saying to ourselves, "I have done something profoundly wrong." When we are experiencing shame we are saying to ourselves, "There is something profoundly wrong with me."

There is a huge difference. Thus, my wife, brought up as a Catholic, could go to confession and be forgiven her sins, and thus have her guilt lifted. Years ago when the president of Toshiba, a corporation as large as GE, came to the United States to express his deep shame after it was discovered one of the small divisions of the company had illegally sold a manufacturing process to the Russians (specifically, a small division located in the Netherlands made a unique grinding machine that manufactured submarine propellers. These propellers allowed nuclear submarines to travel virtually without audible detection). The president of Toshiba felt compelled to resign, not because he had committed an unforgivable sin, but because he had an unpardonable flaw in his character.

The fact is he did not even know this miniscule division existed. Americans still boycotted and demonstrated, as he had not sought forgiveness. Yet, from his perspective, he was seeking to atone for his shame by a far more powerful act, committing career hara kiri. The Japanese did not understand the Americans' protests; the Americans did not understand the Japanese failure to apologize. His actions were totally misunderstood and dismissed.

Let's come back to the question at hand, "How do I deal with the person who comes across as not being able to handle a confrontation?" It is your choice, whether to confront the individual, and in what way; or to avoid the matter entirely. You will need to examine what is going on—within you, with the other person, in your relationship with the other person, and about the overall situation.

Assuming Resilience in People

My experience is that people are amazingly strong and resilient. Indeed, they don't break, even when dropped. The fragility is an act. A wise person told me once: there are no weak people, only emotional blackmailers. The choice to accept the blackmail is yours, not theirs. If the issue is really being forthright, you may be amazed at how well respectfully confronting the other works out. It may not be as hard for either as imagined.

Giving Kudos

And the other side of the coin is also relevant to mention. The fact is we usually associate Straight-Line communication with giving and getting negative input. We all know people who struggle with positive feedback in the form of compliments. Thus, we often withhold it, and this is as harmful in its own way as not giving potentially hurtful information.

Keeping Control When Adrenalin Is Rushing

It must be apparent by now that when God designed us, She/he did so without my advice and to ensure survival. One of the mechanisms to achieve this outcome was the inclusion of a pesky little gland, a mere seven to ten grams, located between the kidneys, at the twelfth thoracic vertebra and near the pancreas. It is called the adrenal gland, and it is the enemy of Straight-Line communication.

When we are afraid or upset, adrenalin starts flowing to the detriment of our logic and invites overreaction (unless, of course, there really is a lion chasing you!). Technically, the secretions are several different hormones, including epinephrine and norepinephrine.

When we become power-aroused, research shows the result is the sort of diatribe described in the opening story of this chapter: an illogical, vitriolic outburst. Among other research findings related to the release of these hormones is the fact that a male who drinks three or more ounces of alcohol will experience the same release of norepinephrine, resulting in lowering what we call "activity inhibition." Simply put, activity inhibition is the part of your brain that controls the impulse to punch your boss (the layman's term is "impulse control") when you are upset with him or her. This is the reason more violence occurs when folks are under the influence.

And while I am on the topic of giving God advice on how to design the human, I might mention the testes and their secretions of testosterone … but enough of that; you get the picture that biology is not the friend of Straight-Line communication for most of us.

What Straight-Line Communication Is Not

I have defined Straight-Line communication as "being open to the point of vulnerability by expressing your honest and complete reaction to what is occurring." I have also stated the goal is to leave the individual or group "more productive or helped."

One of the reasons candor is avoided is due to the many misconceptions about what it is. Many of us, to use the vernacular of one of my colleagues, are "wallowing in our own sh-t," masquerading as Straight-Line communicators. So, while I have defined Straight-Line communication, I find myself in the unusual position of thinking the definition will become much more useful when we agree on what it is not.

Straight-Line communication is not:

- Venting of anger when you are in denial or just unaware that you are upset.
- Dealing with disappointment if you are unaware of doing so.
- Being rude or calling names.

- Being one up/one down; if you are feeling gleeful and victorious after or during the interaction, you were not using Straight-Line communication by our definition.
- Transferring your feelings about someone else or another situation to this person (e.g., I am upset with my performance review and blow up at my wife when she comments on the garage being messy).
- Historical ammunition. Straight-Line communication happens in real time, in the here-and-now; it is not the unearthing of a prior hurt.
- Seeing someone as upset because you are mired in your own issues.
- Blaming or attacking.
- Seeking in any way to get even or to exact a pound of flesh.
- Avoiding dealing with someone else genuinely.
- Shutting down entirely---not engaging.
- A one-way exchange to get an issue off your chest.
- Arguing for the sake of arguing or playing devil's advocate when you're not either, aware of it or, admitting to it.
- Asking a question when it's really a statement.

First, Face Your Own Truth

So, if you have experienced any of the preceding in the name of Straight-Line communication and been hurt or offended, know that this is not the behavior I am advocating or encouraging. I am not saying do not be angry and express it; I am saying if you are angry say so, and do not mask it as Straight-Line communication. Label it as anger, and it will automatically change the conversation for one powerful reason. The person with the anger is the person with the problem. When you recognize you are angry, you are aware you have an issue you are attempting to work through, and you now have at least a chance for Straight-Line communication. If you can consistently express your true experience when you are upset, you have evolved to a higher plane.

The trouble I have gotten myself into when I thought I was using Straight-Line communication seldom came because of my honesty, but rather resulted from my ignorance as to what was really going on with me. I was mistaking integrity for my need to dump my frustration. Somehow, the other person's radar picked up on the fact that I was not acting from a place of integrity. No need to worry; most of us have (again in my colleague's terminology) great bullsh-t detectors. Regardless of whether I was bs'ing myself or them, they knew something was off.

Think about it for a minute: just as you have a built-in compass for recognizing when to use Straight-Line communication, you also know when someone else is not using it. So why would you not give yourself the benefit of the doubt for recognizing when another's input, positive or negative, is meant to be helpful or it is just someone dealing with their own problems? On another note, some may say that being true to yourself is a prerequisite to be authentic.

Authenticity is something that has been explored deeply in professional literature. For example, the reader may wish to review the comprehensive chapter by Bruce J. Avolio and Fred O. Walumbwa that summarizes the integration of the advances in theory, research, and practice associated with authentic leadership, in the recently published *Authentic Leadership Theory and Practice: Origins, Effects and Development*. There is a whole raft of books on authentic leadership, however this is not what this book is about.

In the context of a Straight-Line, being authentic combines two of these concepts. The first concept is the choice to deal with the tough issues; issues no one wants to bring up. The second concept is the vulnerability that people often experience in doing so.

To be authentic is to be courageous. Acting when you are feeling vulnerable is difficult because at its core, it is a threat one feels. The audit trail experienced in the subconscious mind leads us to mental starvation. While this seems absurd on the surface, any psychologist will attest to its accuracy, since we are intrinsically our own harshest critics. Thus, when bringing up the tough issues, at some level, we are concerned that we will be in search of a new position, a new job, in a new company. And I'm not talking about playing devil's advocate here. This is definitely not Straight-Line communication.

Ed Monser's Practical Input:

When Things Turn South

"Using Straight-Line communication starts with being honest with yourself." If you have not yet highlighted this quote in Brad's chapter above, do it now! You must be in touch with your own experience in order to have a chance at Straight-Line communication. The anecdote I will share with you is a perfect example of a group of people who thought they were acting from a place of integrity, but truly it was indirect fear and hostility.

The group running the business unit in question had been, one of the better performing businesses. A successful and proud group, the business had had a strong internal culture before its acquisition, and this culture of pride was propagated with each successive round of corporate change. The business basked in its success and stubbornly refused any outside help on how to run things, particularly from corporate leadership. While they were performing well, this attitude was largely tolerated. But when things turned south, the corporation's executives started paying closer attention to the business's leadership.

Consisting of two product lines making important electrical equipment for industrial applications, this business had a strong grip of the global market share for its products—until the technology started shifting. Companies in Japan came up with a new, more efficient way of making the same products. Their forte had been that their equipment was the utmost in reliability, but the Japanese came out with a design that promised somewhat less reliability in exchange for better power efficiency, and at a lower cost.

Their guys could not believe this would be a successful product approach, clinging to the idea that reliability was everything; and they refused any and all investigation or experimentation with the new technology.

The corporation's executives pushed back, of course, and the group's stubbornness hardened into resentment. They had never taken any outside direction in the past and did not want to start now. When challenged, this group wouldn't fight back and, instead, offered only sullen silence to the corporation's inquiries. The leadership figured that if they simply refused to respond to corporate questioning, the issue would disappear and they could continue doing things their way.

Of course, the new Japanese technology caught on. Customers liked paying less for the equipment and less for the power needed to run it, and they were in fact willing to give up a little reliability to gain these other advantages. They watched their market share get cut in half in two years.

Desperate for answers, the division took an internal audit of the sales team— also frightfully behind, as it was designed to serve the older technology and did not have the appropriate relationships to sell the new product. The corporation prodded for new talent to bring in new sales relationships. Yet, instead of getting up to speed quickly, the sales team procrastinated, always claiming they were under-resourced—when the truth was they were simply slow, stubborn, and unwilling to change.

Simultaneously, their internal business system—created in the 1960s and unchanged since—was a mess. The corporation called for a complete systems replacement from the IT department. Again, the people assigned to it did not have a reputation for being willing to work hard or have the skills to do the work. When questioned, they would say, "We don't have the resources"— when the truth was they were (like their counterparts in leadership and sales) slow, stubborn, and unwilling to change.

The corporation was confronted with deliberate, repeated failure on almost every level of the business. That they did not have the resources to make the requested changes was untrue. That they were avoiding Straight-Line communication with themselves about the dire position their business was in is a much more accurate description of the situation. Because they were unable to get honest about their reality, they were paralyzed by inaction. It got to the point where it was impossible to remove the behavior without removing the people who behaved that way.

The corporation stepped in, they ripped out the stubborn, sullen leadership, and brought in new teams to run the business. Knowing that they couldn't afford to develop the technology internally, they acquired another business that was working with technology similar to the Japanese and integrated their leadership into the product development team. The entire internal system was replaced, and the sales team was updated.

Make no mistake about the ease to this transformation: these changes took almost three years and cost loads of money. It would be a challenge to climb back to the percent market share they once held. However, because the leadership in charge has no illusions about where they stand now—Straight-Line communication prevails within themselves about the present reality and past mistakes of the business—and this number is not impossible to achieve (and perhaps even surpass!).

Chapter 4

The Innocent Question

"I have learned to use the word 'impossible' with caution."

-Werner von Braun

The answer struck me like a bolt of lightning in the middle of the staff meeting. Like most discoveries, it was obvious in retrospect. The perplexing problem that had been keeping me awake for six weeks was finally solved.

I had been retained by a $2.5 billion corporation to work with their number two executive. I will call him Bob. As President, Bob was heir apparent to replace the CEO. He had all the requisite pedigree and was extremely bright and successful by any measure. But, he had a perceived Achilles heel.

The vague assignment was to help him become "more effective with subordinates." While the CEO and his Board had only one reservation about Bob, it was a serious deal-breaker to his promotion. Few could articulate their hesitations exactly, but word was spreading that his subordinates, who liked him personally, did not like working for him. This was made abundantly clear by the resignation of a very talented CFO. The CEO stated firmly that he could not turn the reigns over to someone who could not keep a loyal and motivated executive team. My investigation into the situation began by meeting with all these players individually.

A brilliant strategic thinker, Bob was demanding but fair. He had been aware there was a problem for some time, but it had never gotten in the way of a promotion. For that reason, he was never motivated to get to the underlying cause or move it up the food chain of his priorities.

He was certainly committed to dealing with it now. While he was uncomfortable with the idea of confronting this issue, he understood the potentially disastrous consequences of not fixing this flaw.

In speaking with Bob, I experienced him as honest and he spoke with candor as he attempted to get to the root of what caused the mistrust his staff experienced. In the interviews I conducted with both his present staff and phone calls with past employees the recurring concern was "trust." When pushed, not one person could come up with an example of him not being truthful. However, there was clearly a perception that he was out for himself and not to be trusted.

This was beyond him. His focus was on the tasks he had worked on: he had performed better than most, he met his commitments, and he achieved his goals. When things did not work out it was never because he had not done his part. Because of his track record, he could not conceive of anyone not trusting him. I knew the issue was not in the "content" arena. He was searching diligently in the wrong place.

I looked carefully at all the tricky "mannerisms" which usually account for this type of issue. They are well documented under the topic of 'body language.' These subtle physical cues are often accurate and usually interpreted at the subconscious level. The ability to read these indications is a trait shared by good negotiators and poker players alike. For example, rolling the eyes is universally and correctly interpreted as disrespect, and avoiding eye contact indicates an abuse of truth. (The problem with these tools is simple. Reading one book or article does not create expertise and too many laymen are declaring insights based on spurious data and gross over-interpretation.) With Bob, however, the telltale signs that communicate lying were not present. In our personal interactions, I found him very credible and yet unless we got to the bottom of the conundrum, his career was limited.

He prided himself on not suffering fools. Was the fact that he confronted his staff without pulling punches the cause of the problem? If so we were chasing the wrong issue. In an effort to get more data on this I "shadowed" him to witness how he interacted. This simply translated into attending meetings, observing him on his calls, and joining in on a few business lunches. Truthfully, I was not getting much helpful insight.

It hit me like a hammer at the staff meeting. The topic was a tough one.

He was probing deeply to get a better understanding of how to maintain their advantage in a very competitive industry. His intense line of questioning for clarity and specificity was making his staff very uncomfortable.

At one point, he turned to a vice president and asked, "Do you really think you should have delegated that to Paul?"

The light went on. Every time I agreed with a conclusion he did not say so directly. Rather, he asked a question. When he asked, "Do you really think you should have delegated that to Paul?" the reality is that he was not asking a question but rather, stating his belief that Paul was not the right person to do the work—and everyone in the room sensed it at some very deep level. Instead of confronting a potential conflict in front of others, Bob was hiding his beliefs behind a question.

In our one-on-one meeting, he very articulately stated his positions clearly. Pushback was expected and respected. But in a team meeting I had never seen him do so. It was almost as if you had to guess whether or not he had a position. I will guarantee that each person in the room knew there was almost nothing he had not thought through deeply and had a strong belief about. The result was that his staff often felt second-guessed (indeed, sometimes attacked) but didn't know how to respond to the non-question.

Questions are designed to serve one of two purposes. First and foremost, questions gather information. Second, they invite an individual to think about a topic. (And at the end of this section I will discuss a 3rd purpose questions serve. It may surprise you and is a huge aside, worthy of a book itself.)

By that definition, many of the "questions" posed in meetings are not questions at all, but rather statements masked as questions. In these instances, any attempt to respond will have difficulty dealing with the unspoken issue. Due to Bob's position as President, his constant references to his candor, and his obvious intelligence and expertise, his staff was not consciously aware that their judgment was being called into question. They simply felt something was wrong without being able to put their finger on it.

Once it dawned on me that Bob habitually substituted a question for an honest statement, the intervention was straightforward and powerful. I interrupted the meeting with a comment which in other circumstances may have been rude. "So, Bob, do you have a question, or do you have a statement?" The room looked at me confused. Annoyed at being pulled off topic but used to my abrupt style, he asked what I meant. I then simply repeated the last five strong positions he had couched as questions in the past ten minutes.

I further stated in my experience this was his approach to making his points in groups. I pointed that this violated his much-touted claim to being forthright and it was not an honest approach. To say he was amazed was an understatement. During the next fifteen minutes the executives chimed in. They all stated this was a huge problem for them but that they had not recognized the issue until it was articulated.

This was particularly confounding because of the strong positions he took with them individually. It is hard to agree or disagree with a question, and so it seemed like he was always "setting them up." They felt at risk during these meetings because they never clearly knew what to confront. The impact of this approach was the fundamental cause of his communications/trust issues with his employees.

Many years prior, Bob took on this approach at the suggestion of a well-intended high school teacher who had observed him in team settings. Bob often came to the answer more quickly than most and blurted it out. It did not endear him to others and the teacher suggested a more skillful way to work would be to put his answer in the form of a question. He was impressed that this technique made him more likeable with his peers almost immediately.

Now, by consciously rejecting this ineffectual message and by setting up new norms for how and when to employ questions, Bob was able to repair the trust issues he was experiencing with his staff. He was extremely good at living up to these new parameters and his staff assisted this shift by being the gatekeepers. That brings us to the role of questioning in STRAIGHT.

I have come to the sad conclusion that upwards of 90% of the questions raised in meetings aren't questions at all. They are statements. As such, not only are they masking a STRAIGHT expression, they prevent others from honestly stating their positions, too. While I recognize the value of questions, I must caution that when being STRAIGHT, they are NEVER substituted for a statement of fact or opinion. They can easily be the next sentence ("So, what are your thoughts on that?") but without your expressed statement (or an admission that you have a strong position you would rather hold until you have heard what they have to say), this practice comes at great risk.

As mentioned previously, there is third purpose for questions besides gathering information and eliciting thought: affirmation. This is indeed a category unto itself. We have all experienced a colleague or subordinate leaning on our door and asking, "Did you see my report?" or, to use a blatantly sexist example, a significant other asking, "Does this dress make me look fat?"

These are a unique category that reveals the questioner is in need of an affirmation. They are fishing for a positive stroke. This presents a choice, regardless of your opinion; will you help them get whole? By that I mean, will you help fill them with positives? If so, the only possible answer is to communicate, "You do great work." Or "I love you." Any attempt to address the stated question that does not communicate these points will miss the mark--and you will know it!

Straight-Line Communication versus Trust

As you are aware, this is not a book about trust. The reason is twofold. First, there are already several excellent and compelling books on it, and it has been explored in depth by experts who are both thorough and articulate. I have very little to add that would be beneficial. Second, people often mistake trust for using Straight-Line communication and assume you need a trusting relationship as a prerequisite. While it is certainly easier to use Straight-Line communication when you have a trusting relationship, I maintain the exact opposite is true: using Straight-Line communication is the most potent causation of trust. From my perspective, Straight-Line communication is a prerequisite for trust.

Years ago, I received a call from an individual I had met at a friend's birthday party. He had asked what I did and showed some interest, but before the end of the conversation, the talk had mysteriously turned to how most folks are underinsured. He had thrown in a few examples of folks like me for whom he had remedied the situation. He had seemed very knowledgeable and left it at that.

When I got this call a few days later asking if I would like to play golf as he wanted to get to know me better, for some reason, I found myself putting him off. I like to play, but something in the back of my mind indicated this just did not seem right. Talking with my wife at dinner, I got in touch with the problem I was having.

The reality is, he wanted to sell me insurance. I knew it, and he knew it. If he had only used Straight-Line communication about his intent, we might have gotten to the point of seeing if I needed insurance; and, if I did, would I buy it from him? The fact that he was not fully upfront about his motivation left me not wanting to spend an afternoon with him. Had he simply said, "I would like us to get to know each other better because I'd like to have a discussion of whether or not you need my product," I would have welcomed the game. The lack of trust this engendered by his lack of being up front about his true goal actually hurt his chances of working with me.

Others who have heard this story have challenged me and asked, "What if all he really wanted to do was get to know you better?"

If that were the case, he would not have been the successful salesperson he was. The dominant concern of great sales people is not establishing relationships for relationships' sake but, rather, having an outcome that forwards their achievements. And that does not in any way make them bad people; it just means their wiring is a little different from those whose end goal is the relationship.

And I, like you, have a built-in B.S. detector that is pretty well refined.

Ed Monser's Practical Input:

The Long, Hot Summer in the Desert

Buying large automation equipment and especially custom machines is always an adventure. Often times this equipment is also in the critical path for the introduction of major new products, so the complexity of the equipment and the pressure of an introduction schedule often generate some intense situations. I led a team responsible for the procurement of a chemical etching machine that is an excellent example of this process and resulting stress. And, this will also help to show that Straight-Line communication does not require a high level of trust.

The process to buy the chemical etcher had a detailed front-end where multiple vendors put forward proposals that gave their design, performance specifications, price and very importantly the expected schedule. After many discussions and visits to the various vendor factories, we decided a company we had not worked with before in Arizona had the best overall package and had guaranteed the ability to hit our aggressive schedule. They said they had the technology needed, their engineers were available to start the project immediately, the price was competitive, and it was clear that they really wanted to demonstrate to us, and frankly to the industry, that they could deliver as promised.

Everything started off well and the weekly updates that were emailed in each Friday morning detailed the results from the week and the needed goals for the following week to meet our nine-month delivery schedule. They had assigned a project manager on their side who was coordinating all the needed activity and was the key contact person for all communications. We had worked on the project from the beginning with this manager, so he understood all our issues, and we felt he understood all of us, especially after the multiple meetings and dinners we had during the evaluation phase. The key, of course, was we trusted him. We felt he was technically competent with the etching process, was reliable when he made a commitment to meet or provide information, and we felt we knew him more as a friend than a mere manager. We also liked the fact that he had a keen self interest in the success of the project since it was a high priority for the vendor to prove to the industry that they could deliver.

At the three month point we had a scheduled visit to Arizona to check the overall progress and make some key measurements on the machine to make sure everything was on track. Armed with all the provided weekly reports we felt we were on top of all the issues and were optimistic that things were good to go. Once we got to the production floor, things started to change. The first thing we noticed was the pump needed for the process was different than the one we had specified and different than the one reported in the weekly summary. When the project manager was questioned about the pump he said the specified pump's lead-time was too long, so he had approved an alternate pump for the process. When asked why he did not mention that in any of the weekly reports he said he was sure it would work and that we would not mind. Unfortunately, the substitute pump did not have the quality nor the performance needed, so we had to mind.

The issue quickly emerged that the weekly reports we were receiving were not accurate. A 2X4 was required. My job changed significantly. I now had to take on the difficult task of insuring all the facts were stated openly and accurately. As you can imagine this caused a great deal of discomfort and distress.

I called my boss and gave him the update and the concern. His response was not a surprise when he said, "stay in Arizona till I could guarantee the schedule would be met!". This turned out to be one very long, very hot summer in the desert. The only solution was to use Straight-Line communication with verification of each issue if this machine had any hope of being on time.

I finally had to go to the upper management of the vendor and level with them on all of our findings, while seeking their help in resolving the issues. They put in the required changes. Fortunately, with the Straight-Line communications in *place the machine was completed on time, and I got to go home with the machine when it was shipped. And importantly, a $800M new product line got introduced as scheduled.*

Chapter 5

The Message or the Messenger?

"If you speak the truth, have a foot in the stirrup."

-Turkish proverb

"If you can't do the job, I will find someone who will!!"

I recall this conversation like it was yesterday. It was the statement of a very frustrated CEO, who was demanding a change in sales channels from his VP of Sales. The VP agreed that the change had to be made, but was predicting a 20% revenue drop, if they insisted on shoving it down the organization's throat in the time frame being allotted.

The rest of the organization was also predicting the confusion and reassignment of accounts that was going to wreak havoc with the projections. The CEO just did not want to hear it, and so was attacking the bearer of the bad news.

The scene was pretty ugly with attacks and accusations of unforgiveable management malfeasance. The question facing the VP was simple: should he roll over and agree that the sales would not be hurt, knowing in his heart of hearts he would be doing so at the expense of being honest? Or should he commit to doing his best but with the caveat the CEO did not want to hear?

The issue was not the interpersonal communications style; instead, it was the response itself—he had given the wrong one, and the CEO desperately wanted a different answer. And thus, the CEO was shooting the messenger: a practice with dire consequences.

When conflict arises between two parties, such as in the example above, one or both sides are often blamed for poorly communicating their particular position. While this may be true sometimes, what I've often witnessed instead are conflicting expectations. In other words, if the content is not what we want to hear, then focusing on skillful and effective communication will not resolve an impasse. Thus, in these instances, observations such as "you need to be a better communicator" represent an inaccurate diagnosis of the problem, and therefore a prescription that cannot possibly deal with the underlying issue.

Those are exactly the types of situations I am often called to help address — when the issue has been misdiagnosed. All too often, when a manager communicates a well-thought-through decision her employees do not want to hear, she is labeled a "poor communicator." When this happens consistently, one of the unintended consequences is to squash the honest expression, or the willingness to make hard calls. This brings us to one of the most difficult concepts to grasp, and the least thought-about pieces of the constructs we will review in this book.

Relaying unpopular information (often the result of conflicting expectations/goals) is part of Straight-Line communication. Please review the matrix below. The top two quartiles are problems for the receiver, independent of how skillful you are as a communicator. Regardless of how skilled the VP had been as a communicator in stating their reasoning to the CEO at that moment, the CEO just did not want to accept what he was saying. This put the exchange in the upper right quadrant—effective communicators but low receptivity to their words (see Figure 5.1 below). And so, the CEO attacked the messenger, as often happens in such situations.

Figure 5.1
Message Content Versus Delivery

Here is where it gets a bit complex. What if the CEO were actually angry because he had been late to the meeting (he had a hidden agenda), but he was either in denial of this motivation, or not even aware he was just being vengeful? This is not Straight-Line communication (see Chapter 3: "What It Ain't"). Such confusion comes forth because that example would not qualify to fit on the grid. By definition, to fit on the above matrix: the message, regardless of how difficult for the receiver to accept it, must be generated from honest experience.

Difficulty of Forthrightness

This brings us to an unpleasant reality. One of the reasons we avoid Straight-Line communication is that we are afraid of the consequences of quadrants 1 and 2. If the other person or group has conflicting goals, or will just reject your input, the exchange is predictably going to be a problem; regardless of how correctly you have articulated your position. Thus, you are condemned before you start. And who, except a sadist, would ever enter that type of debate?

There is no way to do a wrong thing right. The wrong thing in this case is to not be forthright about your true reason for taking the position you do. However, in most of these cases, we are dealing with opinions and beliefs, rather than facts. There may be a legitimate disagreement. In the simple example of the projected drop in sales, this was a discussion with both fact and opinion - in short: a judgment call.

One of the macroscopic reasons for not using Straight-Line communication is the fear that there is a line of demarcation, that if crossed, there is no recovery from. Specifically, if I push the wall too far, I will be ejected or rejected. And I do think each of us has such a line. But I also think most of us misjudge where this line is.

Figure 5.2 below, illustrates this concept.

Figure 5.2
Perceived Line of Demarcation

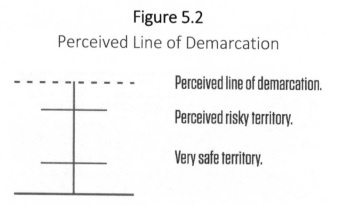

Perceived line of demarcation.

Perceived risky territory.

Very safe territory.

We think of it as far closer to where safety lies than it really is. Since the consequences of crossing this boundary are so dire, we don't risk even that line. Yet the line for most of us is farther out than we realize.

Figure 5.3
Actual Line of Demarcation

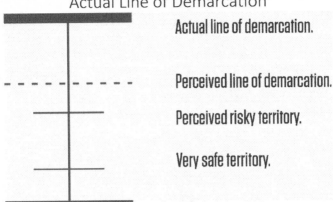

Actual line of demarcation.

Perceived line of demarcation.

Perceived risky territory.

Very safe territory.

Therefore, if we venture closer to the real line, we are still safe and more likely to make a difference in the dialogue. Combining this seldom thought through construct with the quadrant on skilled communicator/tough issues, makes for a more potent understanding of why we don't practice the concept, even when our gut tells us it is the right thing to do.

The bottom line is this type of disagreement occurs all the time in industry. In fact, problems are seldom handled in a straightforward manner. Instead, they usually pass in silence. In this case, your obligation is to express your complete experience at the risk of being vulnerable, and then ensure you hear the other person's perspective on the issue. This will not solve the Palestinian question or make you popular, but the closer you can get to the upper right-hand corner - being skillfully forthright - the less likely you are to be stuck with lasting rancor. The worst place to be is not on the graph, because by definition, that is not even attempting to use Straight-Line communication. And we now know where that road leads us.

The question is not how to speak up about your projected sales or budget projections. Those set targets and actual results are known facts. And while unpleasant to raise at times, the reasons for the variances—and not the goals—are the points for disagreement. A more typical business analogy is when managers are looking to parse the bonus pool. Often when the allocation of these funds is discussed, it is not done in a forthcoming manner. Instead, each person presents a case to maximize his or her benefit, and with not so hidden agendas. Thus, those giving input are not on the grid because they are not using Straight-Line communication in the first place. But even when they are, the temptation to walk on eggs and remain in the lower two quadrants is often overpowering.

Openly Receiving the Message

A whole different and unrecognized problem exists around this issue. The systems in our corporations are not well prepared to address the vertical axis, our ability to truly hear the message. Little in our background has led us to think through our receptiveness, or even to identify it as the problem to engage. Thus, we don't even attempt to dig in and solve it.

Deciding to Use Straight-Line Communication

One of the questions I have struggled with that I am asked frequently is "how do I get more skilled at Straight-Line communication?" I have searched long and hard for an answer, and finally decided it is the wrong question to ask. In my experience, Straight-Line communication is not a skill but rather a *choice*. Yes, you can be more skilled in how you discuss a topic, but the topic you decide to deal with is a decision. To deal with undiscussable topics well is a skill, but to choose to bring them up is a decision. It may be an unconscious or habitual decision, but nevertheless, using Straight-Line communication falls into the realm of choice.

All too often, people work hard to avoid the tough questions (quadrants 1 and 2). Staff will routinely talk around a subject, but never address the true issue. When we are called in to help solve a problem, the real job is often identifying the tough issue that is being avoided. The clue frequently is the fact that there is palpable tension in the room.

So, if we concentrate on the stated problem, we are assured of a long-term relationship with the company, as problems will remain. We will deal with a succession of challenges, fixing each symptom, but all avoiding the real issue. However, when we introduce and use Straight-Line communication, the previously unstated problem comes out, and we finally address it. Great for the company. But not so great for our billings since our job is done!

This creates something of a problem for us who teach effective behavior patterns to businesses. The executive-skills industry is not geared to pointing out what is or is not being said in dealing with the tough-to-discuss questions. As a matter of fact, we don't usually know what is being avoided. We are pretty good at sensing tension in a room that is often a result of people avoiding the tough dialogues. That is a different discussion. Once staff members have made a conscious decision to deal with the issues they would prefer were not present, the consultant's job is done. Those in the consulting field know the key to success is in building repeat business. Once an individual or team decision has been made and is being implemented, we are no longer needed.

The derivation of the word "decide" is the same as that of "homicide" and "suicide." All have "cide" as a root, which comes from Latin (*cidere*) and means "to cut or kill." Once you decide to uphold the principles of Straight-Line communication, your decision means you eliminate dishonesty, even when it's the easier path.

When you decide to use Straight-Line communication (staying in quadrants 1 and 2), your behavior and that of those you deal with, change without much additional input. Thus, the incentive to develop a practice to forward this notion is not overly rewarding—at least not initially. And most teams tend to deny they suffer from such a problem in the first place.

Distinguishing Content from Delivery

All our efforts have been aimed at the effectiveness of communication (the horizontal axis). When you closely examine the products of both in-house training departments and consulting companies, you see highly ethical, hard-working, and highly educated men and women in the field of the behavioral sciences - training managers and executives in how to communicate.

Indeed, most in my field have been taught to show clients how to deliver messages more clearly and how to be heard or understood better—in other words, how to improve their overall communication skills. Experience has taught me that our clients are far better served when we add the variables of identifying, delivering, and receiving difficult information.

In regard to receiving information and a true message, most in my field do not address this equally important issue (the vertical axis). I'm sure many of you will agree this is a laudable and much needed goal. In my case, I see the need for this each and every day.

However, this is where the diagnosis leads to problems. When we condemn someone who is a skilled communicator because of "what" he is saying versus "how" he is saying it, we are discouraging Straight-Line communication. Most of us are not in a position to judge whether the offending statement(s) should have been uttered in the first place. We do not have a set of well-constructed processes designed to distinguish between the message being honest but difficult to hear, and the messenger being a bully.

And the exact opposite may occur. We may often mistake employees who only throw "softballs" as good communicators. That is, they talk nicely, say what everyone feels comfortable hearing, and never raise the tough issues - when in fact they're probably more concerned about not sounding rude in large settings such as meetings. As a result, they avoid Straight-Line communication. In the end, they may be great communicators—*but they are not effective because they are only great at dealing with irrelevant issues.*

If you're looking for Straight-Line communication, you must be able to separate the content of the message from the personality of the sender.

When this does not occur—when you fail to separate the messenger from the content of the message—you end up with silence as the default response. Listeners will have learned it is painful to speak their truth, because they are shouted down or in some other way dismissed. In fact, people who bring up difficult but important content are often called poor communicators—even when they are raising significant issues that could lead to terrible consequences if left unaddressed.

Two examples come to mind of where different types of approaches were appropriate. Number one: let me call him Peter.

Peter was a VP of marketing, who had just said in so many words, "we were all idiots and if we would just leave the ad campaign and new product rollout to him, we could go sit by the pool and the company would be better off." We sat there in amazement. I might add that the CEO had come up through marketing and was generally viewed in the industry as being brilliant.

Being the reticent and shy type that I am, I asked the simple question, did he mean to insult us or was it unintentional? He looked at me like I was from Mars and asked what I was talking about? He really did not have a clue. I did something I seldom do, but thought necessary, I turned the room loose on him.

When they were through, he had been badly beaten with a 2X4 and got the point. Subtleties were lost on him. He claims it was a life changing experience, but it took nothing short of a very direct confrontation for him hear and internalize the issues which were so alienating.

I have made it clear this book is not about the way you say something but rather about content, what you choose to bring up and what you choose to leave unsaid. A point I go out of my way to make is that you will be far more impactful if you do have a modicum of "emotional intelligence" in your approach. The fact is that sometimes to get through a 2X4 is in order. A very direct statement that would sound rude to an innocent bystander is by far the best approach.

The second example I refer to, is what I call the "Connie Adjusted Scale." If you met my wife Connie, you would know that I "married-up." (After a D-1football coach had met her, he correctly observed I had "outkicked my coverage.") So, in her case, a very direct style is not necessary and may even hurt your effectiveness when 'giving your complete experience, even at the expense of feeling vulnerable'. I call it the "Connie adjusted scale." Notice the scale is one of "directness," not of "STRAIGHT."

If I make the mistake of thinking a blunt style is the essence of STRIGHT I am going to create a different problem. And if I choose not to be STRAIGHT because of the degree of sensitivity appropriate, my relationship will suffer; and if it is a co-worker, our productivity will also suffer.

The fact is, she is much more sensitive than the VP of Marketing will ever be and that simply whispering something to her is the equivalent of shouting at him. In my experience this all too often becomes an excuse not to be honest. The assumption people often mistakenly make is, that sensitive people are fragile and will break if dropped. If you believe that I have a bridge to sell you. Let me assure you, my wife is an extraordinarily strong woman, but the degree of directness often needed with many of your colleagues, is the wrong instrument with her.

And having said that, when I have backed away from truly expressing what I felt I needed to say for fear of hurting her feelings (or whatever rationalization I was employing that day) there has been a price to pay. The reality is, in the long run the problems we have had because of my crude style have not come close to rivaling the ones we have faced because I was not straight.

The degree of directness varies, and I make it clear to my clients that I will err on the side of "direct." This is the opposite of what most of us have been taught.

When the issues are various shades of grey (as most are) I state them as black and white. The reason I have for doing this is to hasten our ability to "cut to the quick." I ask them to intellectually calibrate these statements on a "Spencer Adjusted Feedback Scale" for the accuracy but respond from their gut to the demand for change. It seems to work. And periodically I need to beg forgiveness. Connie is a saint.

Encouraging Straight-Line Communication

One simple question that will assess the level of Straight-Line communication in your organization is as follows:

If a CEO, executive, manager or anyone else in a position of authority is attending a meeting, can you and your colleagues, in the meeting itself, raise legitimate concerns and objections to his or her decision? If not, then your organization may have weaknesses in its internal communication culture.

Unfortunately, we often end up with communications skills development (in all the varied, well-intentioned, and often highly effective programs) as the corporate answer, without realizing they are addressing the wrong problem. The result is communication training that often inadvertently smothers dialogue that is, at its core, healthy. We learn to speak well—but on a superfluous issue. And because we have discussed the wrong problem, we don't have a solution to the real issue. So, we continue to address the wrong problem. We have merely treated the symptom, rather than the underlying cause, and the pain persists.

On the other hand, Straight-Line communication cuts down on the time necessary to reach the best possible outcome, while simultaneously resulting in greater respect on all sides.

The Just Plain Wrong Diagnosis

"He is a 'piece of work'" If I made any progress with him I would have done more for this company than anyone in the last 10 years." This was the charge given to me by an exasperated CEO.

He was referring to a very bright, "invaluable VP who could not seem to leave a meeting without pissing off at least one of the participants off. And I mean Big Time. Yet he did an outstanding job and everyone knew it. He was too blunt.

I had not met him in person, but certainly knew him by reputation, and must admit to a bit of trepidation at the thought of the assignment. When the meeting day came, and I met with the CEO and the VP to outline the project for the VP, I was amazed at how calmly he took it. If I read him correctly, he was even anxious to get started. This issue was clearly not in his Blind Area and he wanted to do something about it! Usually there is a defensive wall put up designed to say I am not that bad and the last thing in the world you should do is waste my time with a coach!!

In our first one-on-one he asked what I had in my toolkit to help that was not in the arsenal of Dimensional Development Associates, Center for Creative Leadership, the Dale Carnegie workshops, and several other programs he had taken. I was amazed he had these program s under his belt and questioned him thoroughly about what his takeaways were and how he had attempted to apply them.

I took my usual route and decided to do research. In this case it meant shadowing him for several days and through numerous meetings. This important point regarding Straight-Line communication cannot be made without explaining the role he played in the organization.

He was the buffer between the marketing and manufacturing organizations. In short, that meant, among other responsibilities he did the production

58

scheduling. It sounds innocuous enough until you realize the inherent conflict between the two demanding departments.

The marketing people needed huge quantities of new products produced and on the shelves ready to meet the demand pull they had created for the product on day 1. The manufacturing organization had been built around efficiencies for cost control purposes and the incremental expensive molds, overtime etc., to meet the new release demands would mean that once the initial demands were met, they would have extra tooling, layoffs etc., to deal with the ongoing marketplace demands.

Add to that, the plants were in competition to get the business which was based on the past performance of their ability to produce the product on time and at the projected costs. Thus, the marketing goals were in direct conflict with the manufacturing goals. The manufacturing facilities wanted to have him assign the work to their sight for many reasons. Some very legitimate and some having to do with the fact that the Plant Managers were in competition to grow their facilities and when I say there was testosterone and Ego involvement, I am badly understating the fact.

JT (the VP in question) had to make the call as to how much to ramp up the early production and which plants got the work (they would bid on the work and given history and several other factors JT would then decide.) It was in one of these weekly 'scheduling meetings' I was hit by a fact I did not like. JT had just made a decision about where to assign a product when one of the plant managers in the room blew up at him. The attack was personal and vitriolic.

JT had delivered the rationale in a manner that had you been there, you would have said was factual and respectful. I could not have done it better myself. He had a rationale for his decision based on the 2 years of previous on time and cost performance that was not disputed. But it was not what the manager wanted to hear.

The Straight-Line

I was reminded of an exchange I had been privy to years before when my parents had communicated to my older sister that she had to be home from a date at a time she did not want to be home. The scene was pretty ugly with attacks, tears and questions of "don't you trust me?" and accusation of bad parenting. My parents remained calm and could not have done a better job of communicating but the issue was not the style, it was the fact she desperately wanted a different answer.

Both parties left with a feeling the meeting could have gone better and I was once again asked how to address the interpersonal dynamics. The diagnosis did not come from the field of interpersonal-dynamics. It is systems theory and, in this case, the organization structure that created this problem. More training in communications effectiveness would have been a waste.

Peter Drucker, the well-known business author at one point labeled certain tasks "man- killer" jobs. What he meant was that if you fired Joan and hired Mary and then fired Mary and hired Susan and then in 6 month fired Susan and hired Sarah and then....it was not the person but the job design. He also maintained that 96% of errors were the results of a bad system or process and so when you look to place blame on a person you have a 4% chance of being correct. You can quibble with his percentages but if it is only 92% you still have a pretty lopsided playing field. The blame was being placed on JT and the diagnosis was that he was bad a communicator. When I looked into it, he had lasted longer than anyone else in the position but his 4 predecessors had all been drummed out of the role.

What he was being paid to do was make decisions that were by definition going to be difficult for someone to receive. In retrospect, the title should have been VP of NO WIN. To avoid making them would have cost the company significantly because even a week's head start in manufacturing design against tight deadlines could save hundreds of thousands of dollars. The point is that when we don't like the outcome, we often attack the sender and accuse them of all numerous crimes against humanity.

The distinction between someone being straight and delivering a message the person does not want to hear and being straight and delivering the message badly is a permutation on the model that is important to distinguish. Most of us are not in jobs that are as black and white as JT's and demand weekly calls, but if he was not straight the organization would have suffered.

The matrix below is designed to bring this situation a bit more clarity.

It is obvious you need to deal with these issues in very different ways.

Articulating when a message is Straight-Line communication but hard to hear, or the result of conflicting expectations/goals, will change the nature of the dialogue. This takes both willingness and ability to be very discerning and have the awareness that not all conflicts are the result of poor skills.

And to deal with my editor's concern to close the loop, the CEO and VP are doing very well many years later, because they recognized the real issue and dealt with it.

As for JT (second example), when the CEO realized that the incentives for marketing and operations were not aligned, and their goals were conflicting with JT caught in the middle, we had a long dialogue at his staff meeting with the senior players. They each realized they were attacking the messenger and not the message and that JT was in a no-win position. We also realized that JT was very blunt, and while this was a goal to work on, making him the best communicator in the world would not resolve the issue and the company had to own that they had to address a 'systems problem' not an interpersonal dilemma.

Ed Monser's Practical Input:

The Rest Are Crap!

We came extremely close to turning a massive company success story into a much-delayed success or at worst a disaster. If we had recognized and used the construct from this chapter, it would never have occurred.

Our best product line was under attack. Our major competitor had come out with a new product that was a breakthrough in technology and had superior overall performance. As a result, our largest and most profitable product line was dropping in sales and orders, and quickly losing market share.

We had little choice but to respond with a new technology breakthrough of our own and respond quickly. A new team was formed and was tasked to deliver a complete new product in 14 months, with a stated goal of shipping 100 units to our top customer in that time frame. Everyone on the team knew the goal and knew how important it was to meet the goal. The loyal customers were promised delivery of a product that would surpass the competitor's performance and value.

The normal project time needed for an effort like we were taking on would be 28+ months, so we needed to do things differently, and be prepared to work whatever hours and days needed to deliver on time. To help keep the team motivated and focused, the company decided to highly incentivize the team with a shared bonus. If we delivered, everyone on the team would be rewarded with the largest bonus anyone of us had ever received. And, by the way, it would renew the company's competitive position in the market.

The team was organized in sub-groups. Every week each sub-group reported to the other groups if they were on schedule or not. Cross group communication was excellent. Anytime one group might fall behind, the other groups would move to help out and make up for whatever was needed to get back on schedule. Peer pressure was at a maximum because being late was not an option.

After tons of hard work by everyone, we finally reached the day we all had targeted. After 14 months, we all came together to witness 100 brand new units getting loaded on the truck and drive away. We had done it! The new product was awesome and an excellent answer to our competition. And, we all knew we were going to get paid, and most of us were looking forward to taking our prize home to share with all the families that had made significant sacrifices to support us.

As the people started to drift away from watching the truck carry our prize new product down the road, the head of Test & Quality came over to talk. I put out my hand to congratulate him, easily one of our hardest workers, but he pulled back his hand and looked down at the ground. I was immediately confused and asked him what was wrong. He responded "Do you want to know how many of the 100 units met specification, how many would turn-on, and how many would be potential safety hazards for the customer to use? I quickly and anxiously said yes! He paused and said, "Forty-two are good, the rest are "crap".

To say I was aghast is an understatement. And that is putting it mildly. How could this just be coming out now? I had worked with this man for years, why had he not said anything?

We definitely had a culture where quality was supreme, where each individual in the group took ownership of the integrity of the work that was done. It was a mainstay of our competitive advantage. But all the focus, pressure, incentive, and the constant talk about meeting the target to ship 100 units, the quality message was overridden. It was never said to ship "100" that met spec, so the assumption became the number, the number was the goal. The Quality Manager listened carefully to management and his peer group, and the goal of 100 was always talked about, but no direct reference to quality.

He ended up with conflicting goals, meet the goal everyone was talking about, or deliver a message that would have been very unpopular!! He avoided bringing this conflict up in the numerous communication meetings because he was afraid of the consequences. In our run-up to the first shipment he decided to pass on the quality issue in silence.

Fortunately, he did come forward with the problem, obviously a little late in the process, but before the units got in the hands of our customer. After calling the trucking company and getting the truck turned back, I called all the team leaders back to the plant so we could figure out what to do.

Over the years I have woken up many times replaying the events that built up to that day. I really believe the Quality Manager would not have been "shot as the messenger". That said, it is clear he thought so and felt very vulnerable. The most important learning obviously is you can put in all the processes, checks, measures, and governance and still fail. Without Straight-Line communication throughout the organization, any system can be defeated.

In a larger frame of reference, think of the setback that would have occurred had the bad product been shipped. The great press we received and the testimonials which catapulted the new product line into immediate success in the industry would have been muted if not resulting in the opposite. The product quality branding the company had worked so hard to build up and maintain over the years which allowed premium pricing was at risk. All because one man was not willing to take the Straight-Line in a timely manner. I also do not think he understood the serious downside consequences of not making the facts, as unwanted as they were, clear for everyone to deal with real time. His focus was on protecting everyone's bonus, but with the consequences of putting unsafe product in the hands of the customers and the resulting destruction of the reputation of the company.

There are many lessons here for me as a leader. One is the danger of pure numerical goals. Second is the constant need to ask questions for clarity after goals are given to a group. But most importantly, our real goal is to create an environment where people will be honest, even when they are vulnerable.

Chapter 6

The Role of Conflict and Confrontation

"I never did give anybody hell. I just told the truth, and they thought it was hell."

-Harry S. Truman

I recently came upon a very disquieting contradiction to my long-held beliefs regarding Straight-Line communication. In the eulogy of a business partner's father, it came out that this man (whom I profoundly respected) had a deeply held and well-thought-through philosophy about how to handle conflict. I have been struggling ever since.

Avoiding Conflict

He was a lawyer by profession, as was his father. If I interpret it correctly, he handled most conflict by simply ignoring it because he believed, if left to its own, it would soon be washed away and forgotten. He felt that to rise to the bait only added to the flame and caused harm. Of course, there were exceptions, but they were truly exceptions.

I have thought about this a lot and am troubled that at some level I agree with his logic. It is easy to find the exceptions from large too small. (If you are too young to know who Neville Chamberlain was, look him up to find a reason to deal with conflict when it rears its ugly head. It would seem appeasement does not always make it go away.)

The reason for my consternation is my partner would claim my Straight-Line communication invites, and even causes conflict, and that conflict results in

67

hurt. And I believe he would also add the hurt is multiplied when I use Straight-Line communication, and that I may even delight in the uproar. He might further claim that the conflict (which would not have existed in the first place if I had only held my tongue in cheek) invites further conflict, and if only ignored in the first place would not have been a big deal.

Clearly, if that is the case, a whole lot of rationalization must support Straight-Line communication as the productive and helpful process I claim. Let me repeat how much I held his father in esteem and respect the views of my partner. Unfortunately, they contradict my whole thesis and, if true, suggest that some portion of this book is a waste of time. I do not dismiss this view lightly.

Thinking this through as non-defensively as possible is tough for me. My response might, indeed, be empty rationalization or firmly supported justification. But I must leave that up to the reader to determine.

Three Types of Conflict

In considering the proper reaction to conflict, we must define the term. The conflicts I deal with fall into one of three arenas. The first is the most common in industry: conflicting goals. The second is a close cousin, the failure to meet expectations. (In well-run companies, this translates into missing clear goals. In poorly run companies, it translates into missing ethereal targets.) The third is deeper and much more difficult to deal with: differing values.

(As an aside, there is a popular theory that maintains you should never hold an expectation of anyone else. This is simply a setup for disappointment and estrangement. This may be true from an interpersonal expectation frame of reference, but as a leader in business, you must establish high standards for performance. This is a distinction between setting expectations around goal attainment versus expectations around behavior patterns.)

In my experience, the day-to-day conflict in most business settings usually relates to the first or second types illustrated above. Interestingly, the energy often dissipates when it becomes clear there are simply competing goals, and the questions are not personal. That is because when the parties can dissociate and not personalize the issue (not always an easy task), the nature of what is occurring is suddenly not an attack. When one comes to realize just how few issues are personal, it is truly freeing and invites a greater candor.

The family-related questions I am most often invited into are often a convoluted combination of the second and third conflict varieties. This is entirely misunderstood, and often is deeply subconscious, so that the presenting conflict has very little to do with the real issue. These are obviously more difficult to resolve by a large magnitude. The first thing that must be done is to get to the bottom of what the real issue is, precisely because the parties involved are (often unwittingly) not using Straight-Line communication with themselves.

Keeping Straight-Line Communication Impersonal

Conflict has a way of being viewed as an attack. Straight-Line communication is simply stating your frame of reference fully and completely in a search for a better outcome. The problem with my theory thus boils down to how to use Straight-Line communication in a manner that guarantees the receiver does not personalize it as an attack. Depending on the recipient, the attack will be experienced as honing in on one's competence, personhood, or values. These are hard not to personalize.

My perception is that my partner's father made it through life without some of the headaches I seem to get, and perhaps, I cause. I am still convinced that using Straight-Line communication will avoid much more of the misunderstandings that lead to interpersonal problems than it results in, but with the caveat that it be de-personalized.

Having said that, if we trivialize this caveat, we do so foolishly: it is far, far easier said than done. My partner's father was probably correct that the pain that becomes exacerbated by Straight-Line communication is partially avoidable by simply ignoring it. The tradeoff is an opportunity to make a relationship stronger has been missed to avoid the remote possibility of a rupture.

Confrontation versus Conflict

I really think the point he was making was not about conflict at all but about confrontation. Is it possible to use Straight-Line communication and not be confrontational? The question is another troubling question for me. If the answer is no, then Straight-Line communication will always result in unpleasant tension—at best.

Let's first examine what confrontation is. Confrontation results from having to face an issue you would rather not or having a disagreement that is experienced as unpleasant - or at least uncomfortable. Confrontations occur in all shapes and sizes, but all have in common that a disagreement is being aired head on. The type of confrontation that comes to mind is a stereotypical New Yorker blowing up at a ticket agent because the flight was cancelled. The venting is an honest letting off of steam, but at an innocent victim. Everyone within earshot is uncomfortable at the undeserved abuse, and just wishes the jerk would shut up.

Going back to "what it ain't," you will quickly recognize that this type of assault out of anger is not defined as Straight-Line communication. This is not what we mean when we ask the question, "Are confrontation and Straight-Line communication two sides of the same coin?" Much to my chagrin, I think they are in the same family, as it does start with unpleasant tension most of the time.

As documented previously, the threat of an unpleasant reaction to confrontation's tension leads most of us automatically to avoid it. Inviting this tension is not something done in polite company. Yet not to risk the downside of the tension is to deny the benefit of the resolution, and the probability of a closer relationship and speedier decisions, which will stick. And just maybe, if the conflict were aired earlier, we would not need as many lawyers to help in the resolution.

The Straight-Line

Ed Monser's Practical Input:

Survive the Meeting

Over the years it has been very interesting watching the evolution of Straight-Line communications in various business meetings. One such meeting is where a group of senior corporate leaders meet the leaders of the businesses with the purpose of discussing the changes in the market and business situation in a small group environment.

Fifteen years ago I was the newly appointed Chief Operating Officer. I was looking forward to attending this meeting with this select team of talented individuals. But a few hours into the meeting, I sensed something very off. The various corporate representatives had plenty to say. The business leaders were completely silent; they would listen attentively and take notes, but they would not contribute, question, or challenge a single word being said by corporate. I was shocked. These leaders got where they were because of their capacity for great technical knowledge and business insight, so why was the communication so one-sided? Halfway through my first meeting, I took one of the business leaders aside. We had developed a good relationship over the years with Straight-Line communication between us, and I knew I could trust him to provide me with an honest answer. His explanation was simple: they had been trained by the previous corporate leaders to know if they responded or asked questions, they would get more work—and more scrutiny! They already had plenty to do and weren't looking for tougher goals and more rigorous scrutiny on the ones they were presently tasked with. Their intent was simply to survive the meeting. The leaders had learned that the best thing to do was just sit there, and corporate took this as an implicit agreement with their ideas. The only problem? At the next meeting, the corporate leaders would be disappointed that their requests had not been met, and the business leaders would defend themselves by noting that they never actually agreed to any changes.

An example of "surviving the meeting" occurred when we were reviewing the company's position on the limits of overtime work, a topic with serious implications on worker safety, labor costs, and legal issues. Interestingly, we had data to back up both reducing and increasing the mandated limit. It would have been an excellent debate to see what each of the business leaders, who are on the ground with labor-force policies, believed to be the optimal maximum number of hours. I proposed a policy of thirty hours max per employee per month. No one disagreed—but no one spoke up. The meeting ended.

A few months later, the business leaders turned in their overtime data. Guess what? There was no adherence to the new thirty-hour-max policy. No one had argued against it, and no one had implemented it, either. The basic response was "I didn't say I would do it" (which was true). I was beyond frustrated with the conflicting goals the two sides took into this meeting. Since our goals were not the same, there was absolutely no way to meet expectations. The result? It was months before we settled on a solution for the overtime debate. During this time, we accrued millions of dollars in overtime pay, and more important, the relationship between me and the business presidents eroded. The reluctance to risk a moment of tension meant we did not benefit from an intelligent resolution, until that tension had grown and mounted into an even larger problem.

In all future meetings, each of the business leaders were included on the agenda, and thus the norm became that all were required to talk at some time during the meeting. That coupled with the discipline of asking open ended questions to check for understanding and issues helped to create the environment we were looking for. Continued efforts to create a safe, consistent environment, where participants felt they could speak candidly, resulted in a much better meeting environment. Using Straight-Line communication requires a constant, conscious effort on everyone's part. Regardless of the difficulty in implementing it, the payoff of quicker, smarter results from Straight-Line communication is truly the best path.

The Straight-Line

Chapter 7

I Violate the Principle

"A big man is one who makes us feel bigger when we are with him."

-Anonymous

I recently found myself in the student union at the graduate school where my son had completed a degree the previous year. Conveniently, it has become a habit when staying at a nearby hotel. I now routinely go there to work between client meetings, because the student atmosphere is so stimulating and conducive to work. I ritually get a cup of coffee, go to a corner table, pull out my computer, and innocently blend in (as much as an old guy can). And I am hoping the IQ factor of the area will wear off on me, even a little.

Exceptions to Every Rule

Business happened to bring me there during graduation week and ... **I told a lie.** You see, my son had submitted an essay for something called the "Portrait Project" the year before. It is a contest started years ago by a student that has me still thinking. He simply took the last line of a poem by Mary Oliver and asked his fellow students to address the question it poses: "So what will you do with this wild and precious life?" They had to limit their answers to two hundred words. Each year, about half the student body picks up the gauntlet and submits entries, a few of which are chosen for display during graduation week. My son's response was one featured the preceding year.

As I was sitting in the student union, I thought the Portrait Project might be on display, and I took a short stroll around the exhibit to view this year's winners if they were there. I was pleasantly surprised that they were. I was touring the room when a warm and familiar face recognized me. It was the advisor/sponsor of the project. A delightful woman, she reintroduced herself, and inquired if I had another child graduating.

When she found out I did not have another student at the school, she looked at me in amazement and jumped to the conclusion, "So you came back to see the unveiling of this year's Portrait Project!" The look on her face of pride and delight was irreplaceable. That someone from across the country would be moved to go out of his way to come to view it again enthralled her beyond description. So, I said I was in town on business, had learned the Portrait Project was on view, and had come specifically to see it.

It was not exactly the whole truth, or if pressed, even close. And, you would think I had gifted her a million dollars.

Her devotion to this project throughout the years has taken untold hours of volunteer time. Her realization that someone was so moved the year before that he came back specifically to see the collection brought warmth to her heart that would have been significantly diminished by the reality that my timing was not premeditated.

And yes, I was not using Straight-Line communication because I did not tell the *whole* truth. The fact is, I was delighted the project was up, and I was moved as I read many of the submissions. But it was a boldface lie that I had gone there specifically for that purpose. I assume she will not be reading this work, but if you know her and pass the truth to her, it would diminish the overwhelming joy she experienced when she thought I felt so strongly about her efforts for the project.

Even I believe that sometimes living by the letter of the law of Straight-Line communication is not a gift but a slippery slope. But, your call...

Properly Judging When to Lie

And so why do so many of us fall down the slippery slope in situations not quite so innocent? Most of us convince ourselves there is no harm done, and indeed as with this woman, a miscarriage of grace could be performed that would rob the glory so seldom experienced. This can be very true but is often only a pretense and a rationalization. In the case I stated, I would declare, "No harm, no foul." I would even go beyond that to say, "A good deed was done."

Most of us look at the small oversights to Straight-Line communication that way. I have many examples of the "truth and nothing but the truth" not serving any good purpose and even robbing someone of a possible pleasure. That is not what I am advocating - but take the case of the sauna I so much enjoyed one night with my son when he was still a senior in high school. We had a longstanding habit of deep discussions on far-ranging topics in the Jacuzzi. But on this night, he also joined me for a sauna, which is what I preferred.

We left the great evening with a hug goodnight and a wonderful feeling. Or so I thought. I awoke the next morning to a two-page, single-spaced note that could be summed up in a few words: YOU ARE REALLY FAT. I was hurt as I read it, and when I get hurt, being human, my first response is to lash out brutally at the source. As I reread the letter which was signed "Love," I had to rethink what was happening. My son, a natural athlete, had about 2 percent body fat, and what he was saying in his letter was he was afraid he would grow up, get married, have kids, and I would not be there for them. He stated he had not noticed with my clothes on just how overweight and out of shape I had become, and he was desperately frightened he might lose me.

He went on to say he did not know how to say that to my face in a way I could hear it as helpful, so he was staying up to write me a letter.

Would I have been better off if he had just let the glow of the evening remain? How vulnerable was a seventeen-year-old in telling his father his sedentary lifestyle was wrong? When I came to my senses and realized the intent had nothing to do with being hurtful, I had an interesting choice. Did I need to let him know he was out of line to harshly judge and critique his dad like this? Or did I need to reinforce the guts it took to be vulnerable and express his real response to his experience?

He faced one of those slippery slopes and made (in my mind) the right call. It would have served no useful purpose to have him harbor these thoughts so I could linger in the glow of a great evening. In fact, I think his lack of expressing them would have been detrimental in ways I never would have realized. That he was and is still using Straight-Line communication (admittedly with a good deal more tact than his father), has contributed to our relationship, which is the envy of many of our friends. He knew the right thing to do and decided to take that path, despite the fact that it was the hard road. He did not let the unspoken thoughts bother him but expressed his disappointment and fears in a letter when he could not bring himself to say it in person. As crazy as it may seem, that note remains a chapter in our life, which to this day brings me warm feelings. Thus, what would have been the momentary and long-forgotten sense of closeness emerging from the sauna, has grown into a much more powerful and close feeling, which has had a lasting impact on me (and yes, I weigh less today because of it).

Using Sensitivity and Common Sense

In a discussion I had with an individual about the concepts in this book, he was struck by a recent issue he was facing. A very good friend of his was emailing him daily, with pictures of his new baby. Needless to say, the friend was a proud parent.

The problem was that he and his sister thought the baby to be rather unattractive. They posed the question to me, "Should I use Straight-Line communication and tell his friend I think his baby is not attractive?"

My answer was—and is—an adamant, NO! Remember in my definition I indicated the objective was to leave the person or group helped. I see no help at all in sharing your opinion of a baby's looks when it can only bring pain and there is little they can do to change it.

I probably would not go out of my way to gush over the baby's looks when I was present, but that is just the way I am. Often more is said by what is left unspoken. If asked directly and unable to worm my way out of a direct answer, I have been known to lie outright and give an opinion that reinforced what the other was looking to hear.

The Straight-Line business communication I am describing does not necessarily mean you need to comment on a dress you don't like, or a tie you think is gaudy. This, of course, changes when you strongly believe that it will impact the company's ability to make a sale. The second case in which the comment is called for is when your friend is going on a date and asks for an input. Not being honest is not being kind.

As my long-suffering wife knows, I always love her choice of shoes, and her dress never, ever, ever, ever, ever makes her look fat. But that, of course, is the truth.

Ed Monser's Practical Input:

Does the End Justify the Means?

My introduction to the importance of using Straight-Line communication (and the result of a lack of it) came when I was an ambitious young manager in my division's New Product Development department. We were growing, which also meant everyone was overtaxed with key projects, and it was hard to find skilled engineers and experienced people to staff a development team. Of course, my boss still expected my peers, and me, to form those teams: and get exceptional new products out on time and on budget. I could have worked with the new people we were hiring. But they required so much orientation and training that it would have slowed my projects down.

The company policy dictating how to form teams was to post openings on the division's open-job board and wait for responses. I felt this program was flawed, as did my peers. So did several of the HR professionals who were in sympathy with our staffing dilemma and our new-product demands. But I chose to avoid using Straight-Line communication, and the possibility of being counted against the policy that was hurting the division (and many years later was indeed modified). Instead of complying with this slow HR procedure, I took a shortcut.

Setting about my plan, I identified people with the skills, talents, and drive that would contribute the most and the fastest on this key project, and wooed them directly. I sold them on how they would get to work on a new technology or perhaps win a patent.

It was an arrogant, shortsighted decision. I believed I could prove my value by getting the job done better and faster. But I had no regard for how this tactic would prove dangerous and damaging to my working relationships with my colleagues. Furthermore, it truly did not occur to me that I could lose my job; indeed, my arrogance was such that I believed my value would be proven in getting the job done. And if I were to be fired, I was confident another job was waiting for me around the corner.

My approach worked, and my talented staff completed the project on schedule and with superior results. In retrospect, some of these breakthrough products changed the competitive landscape of the industry. My boss and the corporation were delighted with the results.

But when the other project managers discovered my behind-the-scenes recruiting and called me out, my boss did an about-face. He questioned my ethics in teeing up an unfair playing field. He came very close to firing me for violating the policy. In retrospect, I am not proud of my behavior (firing may have been justified). My colleagues felt burned by my unfair advantage. They had dedicated themselves to working within the system and playing by the rules, and this shortcut upset and unsettled them.

At the time, I was shocked. But, from my current role, I can now understand my boss's dilemma. I had not taken the high road and been honest with him, my peers, or the system: and this put him in a very tough position. Does the end justify the means? If I had only dealt with the real issue in a forthright manner, the division policy might have been revised much earlier, and to the benefit of many.

At the time, I felt the HR process hurt our organization's ability to perform in the rapid time frames the competitive market demanded. We all felt the policies were not serving us well. But rather than using Straight-Line communication, and challenging the organization to develop a better approach, I played it safe.

Now I had no credibility on the subject. I eventually got back on my boss's good side, but I never regained the trust of some of my talented peers, and my productivity on future projects suffered accordingly. Two colleagues refused to work with me and would not talk to me. I clearly remember running into one of them at a local store; he made eye contact, immediately turned his cart around, and skipped to the next aisle. It was hard to repair all the damage. The majority of my coworkers cut me some slack, for which I am grateful. I had to go to each person and sincerely apologize, admitting that we wouldn't work together as a company if we didn't all play by the same rules. I pledged to each that I would adhere to this and asked to be held accountable on this issue. I worked hard to live up to their second chance investment in me.

Indeed, behavior does have consequences. Fortunately, I was not fired, and my transgressions were forgiven by most, but I did take away a lesson on peer relationships and Straight-Line communication that has served me extremely well since.

Chapter 8

If You Can't Say Anything Nice, Don't Say ...

*"There is no such thing as a fragile person, only an
emotional blackmailer."*

-Hedges Capers, Sr. Ph.D.

Phil was beside himself when he called. He was distraught. As the chairman and CEO of a holding company I had been working with for about ten years, he was usually very calm and measured. He was, much to my amazement, considering firing the president of a division that was performing extremely well.

He did not want to discuss the issue on the phone, and if I recall correctly, the call came on a Wednesday morning and he needed me in Chicago to discuss the problem in person before another audit committee meeting the following Tuesday. I rearranged my calendar and arrived in time for dinner on Thursday.

As the story played out, Dennis, the president, had thoroughly embarrassed Phil at a meeting with a new board member Phil had spent two years recruiting. The new recruit was the immediate past CEO and chairman of the board of one of the "Big Three" accounting firms and had raised the stature of the board in Phil's eyes. I agreed, the man added a bit of prestige to this seven-hundred-million-dollar company. The recruit was also a member of one of the clubs Phil belonged to, and a much-respected member of the finance community whom Phil desperately wanted to impress.

Phil told me he was aware the issue might sound petty, but it was truly not a small transgression.

"Any executive who was at all sophisticated should have known better!" he said.

"Knew better than what?" I was dying to ask.

It came out soon enough.

Dennis had been the CFO at a company Phil had acquired about two years previously. The owner had sold it to him with the caveat he would step down in a year, but that he had a very good replacement in Dennis. Phil had interviewed him extensively, including the requisite dinner with their wives. Dennis passed a very important test, the moment Phil's wife expressed she liked both Dennis and his wife very much. Phil's grandfather, who played more of a role in raising him than his own father, was a successful business owner. Phil constantly referred to him as a "captain of industry," and often quoted him. His grandfather had provided him with several rules to live by when it came to running a company. One, for example, was when hiring senior executives - he said, "Always interview the wife."

It turned out Phil had always met with Dennis sitting across from a desk or conference room table. The meeting with the new board member was in Phil's comfortable office, and they ended up sitting on the couch and chairs around a coffee table. That's when it happened.
Dennis crossed his legs. He was wearing socks that did not go "over the calf," which meant you could see the flaking, pale skin on his shins.

One of the early lessons he remembered vividly from his grandfather was that sophisticated and successful executive always wore OTC (over the calf) black socks. Everyone groomed for the boardroom knew this and adhered to the rule. Even with jeans, Phil followed his grandfather's mandate. There had once been two junior executives at the company who did not do this, but they were long gone and not really any good anyway, so they weren't missed.

As I said, Phil was distraught. What must this new director think of Phil for having the president of one of his divisions be so inept as to not wear the correct socks? The new director had grilled Phil pretty hard about some items on the balance sheet that the other directors had not paid attention to. Could this be because he recognized he had employees who were not up to the positions they had been selected to fill? Perhaps a geeky CFO who was brilliant might be able to get away with it, but not a CEO. It reflected so poorly on Phil's judgment to have hired Dennis in the first place.

The fact that the division was performing extremely well, and Dennis was respected by his subordinates and peers, was now weighing heavily with Phil. He tried to explain the angst he felt, while recognizing at some level the offense classified as a mortal sin. He was in pain as he asked if he should fire Dennis, or asked if I would talk to him about the socks? (I could not make up a story like this; indeed, fact is stranger than fiction.)

As crazy as it may seem, I run into variations on this theme often. Chasing the question of the socks would have gotten us nowhere.

The Subconscious Power of Messages

Psychologists have long recognized a very subconscious causation of our day-to-day beliefs, and behavior starts with the early messages we received as impressionable children. I use the term "messages" as technical jargon from the concept of "scripting" in psychology. The fact is that our early socialization comes strongly from our interpretation and acceptance of the inputs we get from powerful people in our lives.

These are labeled "messages." Powerful people are often our parents and grandparents, and we then extend this category to include other authority figures—teachers, clergy, early bosses, etc.

In an effort to influence us to grow up to be successful and good citizens/parents, they imbed, often unwittingly, messages on literally every

85

topic on which, we have an opinion or feeling about today. The source, and even the fact that you have these imbedded predispositions, are always unconscious—unless someone brings it to your consciousness.

Because these came from powerful authority figures, you chose one of two options. You either accepted the message as the gospel truth from an unquestionable source of wisdom or rejected it as part of rebelling against that authority figure. Thus, the tyranny of "either they are absolutely correct, OR they are absolutely wrong" - with little room for gray areas - becomes a powerful determinant of our behavior patterns.

To check the validity of this phenomenon for yourself, simply take a moment and write down the catch phrases that come to mind for each of the following five (it could easily be a list of five hundred) items. For example, if I listed "money," you might write down "a penny saved is a penny earned," "save for a rainy day," or "you can't take it with you." Then attempt to identify where it came from. Often it was not from the actual original expression, but from learning by observing others.

Table 8.1
Potency of Early Messages

Word	Message that comes to mind	Where it came from	Is it true for you today?
Love			
Work			
Sports			
Wealth			
Family			

Potency of Early Messages (above)

Now examine how strongly you believe each message to be true. And then comes the caveat—in truth, how much does this long-ago accepted or rejected message dictate your behavior today?

When you think about it, if you totally rejected the message, that rejection also controls your behavior. The message may or not be objectively accurate, but it is true for you, and that is what is important. It does not speak to how independent or how strong or weak you are but, rather, to the programming process of your brain as you grow.

Phil had an early message about the executive dress code that was deeply imbedded in his subconscious from a very powerful authority figure and source of wisdom. It was unquestioned in its accuracy, because to doubt it would call into question the credibility of his bigger-than-life grandfather. The purpose here is not to question the truth or fiction of the correlation between executive competency and OTCs but rather to put into perspective the potency of this message, and others, which you may hold. I had to help Phil understand the source of the message and redefine the power of this and several other "laws" he lived by, that did not serve him or his company well.

Creating Good or Bad Habits

From a behavior-forming standpoint, what happens in the early brain-development process is referred to as "chunking." When the brain is learning, the work is a bit exhausting. So, it learns in a way that is efficient—it forms habits. This makes life much easier.

For example, think about how much energy it took when you were first learning to drive. You had to consciously think to accelerate around a corner while turning the steering wheel just the right amount, and if you had a manual transmission, making certain you were in the right gear.

After not too long, your neuro-network system connects all the dots so you do it without even giving it a second thought. You can drive home and not be aware of the last ten minutes of driving. Or better yet, it will seem effortless, and your experience will be that it did not take much thought or energy. Often, it is hard even to remember the difficulty you had when first learning.

However, driving through a torrential downpour that requires your each and every move of the steering wheel and gas pedal to be thought through, is exhausting. As any market researcher can tell you, our aversion for what is demanding, and gravitation toward what is easy, is the reason it is hard to get you to change supermarkets and other buying habits. It is just easier (I did not call you lazy) to go back to the same stores again and again and explain it away as they are a better choice. The reality is that you know where the bread and milk are.

That is how chunking works, and yes, our knee-jerk responses as to whether to use Straight-Line communication are the result of this brain-pattern formation. If we have to be conscious of everything, it drains our energy levels rapidly.

With that stated, if we develop these patterns early on, is this a valid reason to resign living with it unchallenged when it is not effective or helpful? More specifically, is it a legitimate excuse to avoid Straight-Line communication?

Are We Fixed in Our Ways or Able to Grow?

I have committed to my editor not to bore readers with the plethora of research around the topics I am raising. I'll limit my exposition regarding this subject to the documented work of a University of Stanford professor, Dr. Carol Dweck (yes, her last name is missing a vowel somewhere).

In a book every parent would do well to have under his or her belt, *Mindset: The New Psychology of Success. How We Can Learn to Fulfill Our Potential* (Ballantine Books, 2008), Dr. Dweck researched (mostly among young students) the question of whether they saw their IQs, skills, and abilities as set in concrete? (She labeled this a "fixed mindset") Or did they view them as developable? (She labeled this a "growth mindset")

The results of her many experiments are counter to the traditional constructs upon which so much of our child-rearing and management practices are based. In short, those students who believed they could change and get better and even smarter on standardized IQ tests did so. The reality is, when you adopt a growth mindset, you can change the patterns you have developed.

Your Early Messages About *Straight-Line* Communication

What early messages did you receive about being nice to others? If your programming is "if you can't say something nice, don't say anything at all," are you stuck with it for life? Perhaps we misinterpret this saying as meaning we should avoid being confrontational, and thus conflict seeking - even if what we say comes from a place of genuine concern for another person's well-being, and a commitment to being honest.

In a compelling application of her concepts, an inner-city school principal adopted the perspective that "your brain is like a muscle" by simply changing the grading system. Students now received letter grades of A, B, C, or NY, the latter rather than a D or an F. The NY stands for "not yet," meaning, "This is hard (like anything new) and you are not stupid; you simply have not mastered this YET. But you can and will if you stay at it, because you can change your capacity." I won't bother to recount the details of the school's outstanding success in graduating its kids and permanently changing their lives for the better.

So where do you stand in relation to your view of your mindset, relating to your ability and skill to grow your *Straight-Line* communication muscles?

Those with a fixed mindset believe they are stuck with one manner of communicating, while those with a growth mindset believe they can change it. The majority of those who grow to leadership positions in major US corporations (in my experience, more so - and less so in other cultures) have strongly imbedded injunctions, that people who are not kind are not good and effective people. Most of us want to be in the category of good people.

Redefining Nice

So, if we are going to deal with deeply embedded messages that came from folks far too wise for us to disagree with, we must take a different tact to have any prayer of being successful. Like a karate master, we must use the other person's force and momentum. Instead of arguing about whether to be nice, we need to examine what the terms mean.

How do you define "nice" and how do you define "kind"?
If you define "nice" as not telling someone what you are really experiencing at the expense of the relationship, then you will never be consistently using Straight-Line communication. This is simply because it would be too much of a struggle to fight against all the internal messages you have received and accepted, as the right and proper way to live your life.

If, however, your mindset redefines the terms "nice" and "kind" to mean helping the other person or group be more effective, by examining another perspective and perhaps being more in touch with reality, then your messages will uphold Straight-Line communication's tenets. This means using your deeply held beliefs to invite these behaviors. It is much easier to relearn your definitions, than question the messages from those we put on pedestals as unquestionable figures (the reason we made them unquestionable is deep and involves our safety, but I digress).

To deal with the definitions, we must go back to the potency of messages. While they are subconscious for the most part, the information actually forms the basis of our self-image. Have you ever noticed those who consider themselves clumsy, trip more and drop more things, than those who consider themselves very coordinated? Their behaviors back up their self-concept.

This brings us to a very important construct that gets little attention:

All behavior is designed to reinforce and enhance our self-image.

What does that mean, and why is it in a book on Straight-Line communication? The fact that if my self-image tells me I am clumsy (far more probably an early message that became a self-fulfilling prophesy, rather than an early lack of coordination), this message causes me unconsciously to reinforce it. Thus, kids who think of themselves as great athletes tend to develop into better athletes. If our self-image is that we are nice and kind people, we will act in ways to reinforce and enhance this image. Of course, tied to that message is the corollary that you will hurt someone when you are using Straight-Line communication, and that is not being nice.

So, if Straight-Line communication is the antithesis of being nice, using the former flies in the face of the self-concept you have so carefully fostered. This self-image powerfully controls much of your behavior patterns that are driven by this unconscious message. Rather than arm wrestling about your self-image (a battle I am preordained to lose badly), or attempting to alter your early messages (I will leave that heavy lifting to you and your therapist) I choose the expedient method of having you reexamine your definitions of being nice - so when you use Straight-Line communication, you will reinforce your well-engrained self-concept.

Thus, one of the major arguments I make in support of Straight-Line communication is counter-intuitive. This simply means it flies in the face of unexamined common sense. My experience tells me that Straight-Line communication is actually the high road to being nice and being kind. Being AVOIDANT is the route to being unkind and limiting your relationships.

Is it nice to let someone walk down the hall with his shirt hanging out of the back of his pants? Is it nice to let a marketing assumption that will determine the pricing (and thus the success) of a new product go unchallenged when you have reason to disagree?

Risking a Negative Reaction

The definition I am using is often confused with being rude or confrontational, and leaving someone embarrassed. If that is the intent, then we are not using Straight-Line communication. However, at times such a negative reaction may be the impact. We must ask, "Is it worth the risk?"

The following illustrates three simple yet profound steps to look at any communication and answer that question:

1. The Intent
2. The Behavior
3. The Impact

The steps look something like this...

Figure 8.2
My Desire in Communication

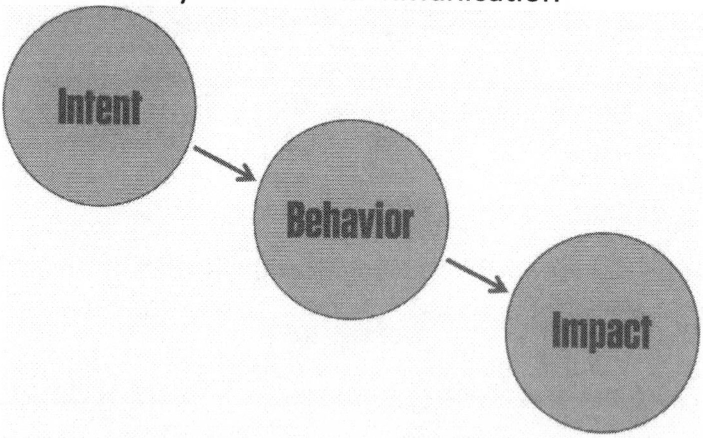

Let me explain. Have you ever said something to someone, and by the nature of his or her response, immediately known the person could NOT have heard what you said? In all probability, you found something happened in the translation of your words, and your intent did not come through.

I have a habit of scheduling important calls from the East Coast early my time (West Coast) and continuing them on my cell driving to the office. I will then put the cell phone to my ear and walk quickly to my office, right by my assistant's desk. Preoccupied, I will wave quickly and shut the door to continue.

My **intent** (and indeed what I think I communicate) is "Great to see you. Hope you had a great weekend with your family. I would love to spend more time talking, but I am tied up right now. Sorry about that."

My **behavior** is to walk quickly by my assistant's desk and grunt something as I quickly close the door to continue my conversation. For as many years as that has occurred, you would think one of us would have learned something. But, alas the following scene occurs again and again.

She will walk in the office when I am done wondering what was wrong or if something disturbing occurred the previous week, genuinely fearful for her job. My **impact** is to invite her to wonder why I am angry with her. I am always flabbergasted when it finally occurs to me that she believes she has upset me.

Figure 8.3
What the Sender Experiences

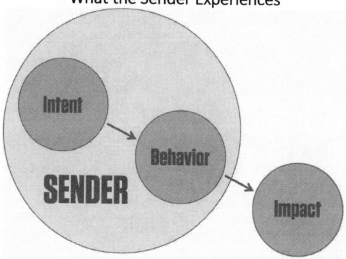

As the sender of the communication, you are able to know your intent, and with any awareness at all, your behavior. But unless you have a crystal ball, you cannot know the true impact unless someone tells you, or you finally recognize something is off in the response you expected from the other end.

Figure 8.4
What the Receiver Experiences

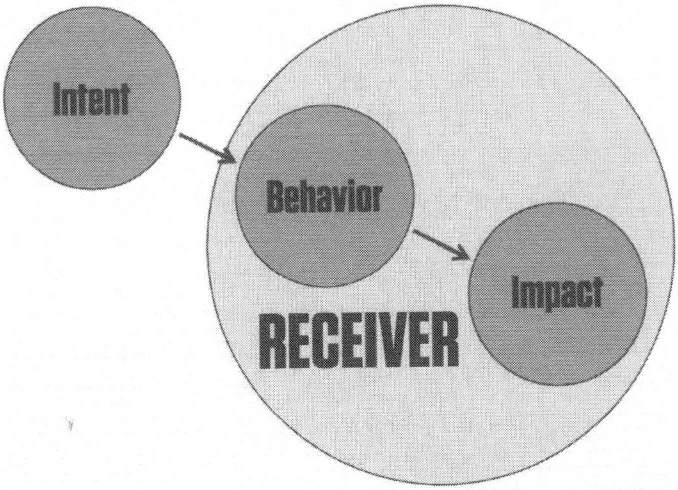

As the receiver, all you are privy to is the behavior and the impact. Unless you have the crystal ball (I rue the day mine broke), you cannot possibly know the intent without checking with the sender.

Thus, Straight-Line communication is often defined by the impact on the receiver, without giving the benefit of the doubt to the sender for trying to be helpful. I suggest the sender focus on intent, rather than impact. If you are going to use Straight-Line communication consistently, you have to define that as the intent. To attempt to act in a way that controls impact is a lofty goal, and if aimed for, should often be thought through thoroughly. Too often, considerations of impact are just excuses to avoid Straight-Line communication. And to illustrate this concept - now the final steps look something like this...

Figure 8.5
The Limitation in Communication

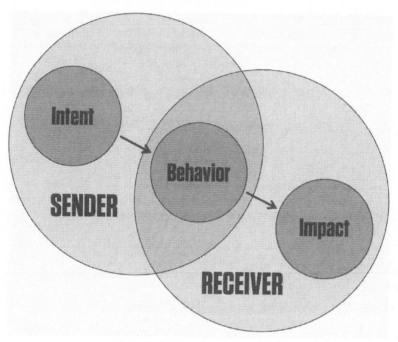

The Role of Apology

Straight-Line communication often has the impact of inviting temporary dislike. What I mean by this is the initial anger will go away (usually more quickly than you imagined), and the relationship will return to its former level, or even improve. Most of us are terrified by any sign of displeasure. So, what do I do when my intent is misconstrued and someone is hurt? I genuinely and profusely apologize and attempt to communicate my intent. I beg forgiveness for the unintended hurt. This may or may not be accepted, but I have found over the years it goes a long way toward my ability to establish and maintain relationships. By the way, if I am not genuine in my apology, it will not improve the situation. As I have stated earlier, most of your colleagues, from janitors to presidents, have what my partners describe as "well-developed bullsh-t detectors." So, if I am not being sincere, I simply dig my hole deeper, and probably deserve the rejection I get.

The positive effects of a sincere apology are evident throughout society. In numerous studies, when a physician initiates a discussion in admitting an error (the legal term is malpractice), the lawyers are left out. Indeed, a genuine mistake is understood as a condition of being human, and with no malice or forethought in the mistake, the tendency across the nation has been to accept the apology and move on. The fear of a lawsuit and the resulting AVOIDANCE or denial has the effect of increasing the probability lawyers will make a lot of money. Straight-Line communication, in this case, seems counter-intuitive. From the amygdala's perspective, when deciding to admit the error or avoid the problem, the mistake needs to be avoided. But the research can lead to no other conclusion than this is not the lobe best used for this critical decision.

While I want to encourage you each to be nice and to do the right thing, I also recommend that you reevaluate your definition of nice. And then you will test my hypothesis that when you do so, your intent will more often be the impact you had fantasized.

Epilogue: "Sockgate"

Once again, my editors have had their say and encouraged me to complete the story of Phil and Dennis. Phil begged not to have to confront Dennis, as he was embarrassed and afraid this quirk would make him look bad in the light of day. I recognized the message was simply too deep not to bother him each and every time they were together and would put serious limits on their ability to work together. I finally told Phil I would carry the message - an unusual step for me.

I immediately walked down the hall to Dennis's office and asked if he would like a piece of feedback that was limiting his effectiveness, but that it was going to blindside him. His response of course was yes.

The Straight-Line

I explained Phil's dilemma, how powerful the message was, and how embarrassed he was about it. I then told him that, like it or not, Dennis was also wired with messages as crazy and that. While we needed to laugh this off, it was funny at a very profound level.

As I knew would be the case, Dennis was not married to the length of his socks. And when I suggested we have Phil take us across the street to Neiman Marcus, and make him buy a pair to his liking, Dennis got into the idea. We marched into Phil's office and with great fanfare announced we had a job for him that was going to be expensive. We ended the day with genuine belly laughs over a drink (or three) at Phil's favorite watering hole, after he had insisted (much to Dennis's chagrin) on buying all eleven pairs the store had in stock.

The sock incident became a standing joke over the years, and on several occasions when they became stuck in a strategic argument, Dennis would threaten to revert to his short socks - and this would break the ice. At a black-tie affair, when Phil was being honored as the City of Hope Man of the Year, he showed up in a tuxedo sporting a short pair as a joke. Phil promptly paid one of the waiters to go to the nearest store and return with a pair of OTCs, which Dennis donned with panache. Once, they even told a version of the story to a baffled reporter who was doing an article on the company's successful growth in the stock market. Straight-Line communication directly led to a deepening of their relationship and interpersonal productivity. I think we know what the end of the nice road of shoving the sock issue under the rug would have been. As I said, I couldn't make this up.

Ed Monser's Practical Input:

It Was the Door

I was running an aggressive new product development program. Our biggest competitor had launched a product that was destroying our market share. We needed a new product, and we needed it fast.

We pulled together an incredible team. These were high-priority people with high-priority talent. Because we only had fourteen months to accomplish what sometimes took several years, we had to develop flawless communication to keep everyone on the same page. One of those tools was a program that could be criticized as micromanagement. It was a weekly Monday morning meeting wherein all team members would explain to everyone exactly what they were going to get done that week. The following week, they would report what they did/didn't get done and how this affected the coming weeks' priorities. The benefit of this was visibility. No one slipped by unnoticed. The program did NOT start out with great meetings.

The first couple of Mondays passed, and I was concerned that the team acted suspicious. People didn't want to point fingers, ask hard questions, or assign accountability to their coworkers. Everyone wanted to play nice, and no one was willing to use Straight-Line communication. But after our meetings, there would be a steady stream of individuals who needed to talk to me. One by one, they would slip into my office and close the door behind them. Then they would spill their guts about all the obstacles and challenges of the topics we had discussed—or tried to discuss—at our weekly meeting! It was a mess. I believed I had created an environment for people to be candid, ask questions, ask for help, and feel safe doing that, but it wasn't working at all how I had envisioned.

It took a couple months before I finally realized the problem: it was the door. It was a Monday afternoon, and the fourth or fifth person walked into my office, closed the door behind her, and began airing out her opinions in the safety (and anonymity) of my office. That's when it hit me. I took a screwdriver, popped the hinges off my heavy wooden door, and carried the fifty-pound thing across the entire office, through the factories, and right to the dumpster. With a great heave, I launched the door into the empty dumpster where it made an ear-splitting noise. I walked back into my office, past dozens of people staring at me in disbelief. The head of the team was still there. "I'm sorry. What were you saying?" I asked.

"I think I need to go talk to my team directly," she said. The next week things started to change.

Chapter 9

Making the Choice

"If a thousand people say something foolish, it is still foolish. Truth is never dependent upon consensus."

-Anonymous

"But I was raised in a family that never confronted. It is just too late to change my stripes," he told me with conviction.

This CEO was explaining why he could not practice the principles of Straight-Line communication and become better overall in the exchange of ideas. I listened (I must admit, less than empathetically), and before the end of the lunch, he had for the first time in his life told the waitress he did not really like the salad. We left only after he had accepted the profuse apologies of the owner and his sincere thanks (it turns out the cheese was rancid and they did not know it), while insisting on paying the check despite the owner's pleading to comp the bill. We had practiced the rules of leveling, I will review later in this chapter.

While the CEO's statement about his salad may seem a very small and non-threatening step, it was a step in the right direction. Every journey begins with a small step, and I can attest to the fact five years later he has come a very long way. His self-reported major gains indicate his personal and business successes, and improved relationships. And he is a favorite at that local restaurant.

We hope it is clear by now that we believe Straight-Line communication is a choice. While it is an often unconsciously impacted choice, nevertheless it is a choice. And whether this CEO recognized it or not, he had and has the power to change his choice.

Yes, there is help at getting more comfortable and more competent at being an excellent Straight-Line communicator. Specifically, there are two concepts that will help those attempting to develop better skills in this arena. In Chapter 3: "What It Ain't," I implied what Straight-Line communication is. Let me be a bit more specific now. In its most lofty sense, **it is taking a perceived interpersonal risk with the lone goal of leaving an individual or a group better off.**

When the goal is to lay someone out cold, this is not what we mean by Straight-Line communication. While striking out in that way may be very satisfying, it seldom helps the other person. When you are simply venting frustration, the benefit is to let off steam. Again, while potentially satisfying, it seldom helps the other person—or you in the long run. If any part of your motivation is to come out of the interaction as the top dog, it is not Straight-Line communication. If your intent is a power play, expect the outcome to be diminished trust and increased defensiveness and hostility.

Straight-Line communication results in greater trust because the goal of being helpful is always present, even if it is not recognized until after the fact. To be most effective, there is a "helping contract" in place, even if it is only implied to begin with.

Self-Awareness

One of the techniques I find helpful in becoming more skilled at Straight-Line communication is the Johari window. This is a communications model developed many years ago by two psychologists, Joseph Luft and Harrington Ingham (1955). Simply put, it breaks our personalities into a four-quadrant matrix. The Y axis is divided into two sections— "what you know about me" at the top and "what you don't know about me" (often the things I may be hiding from you) at the bottom. The X axis is divided into two parts— "what I know about me" on the left and "what I don't know about me" on the right. (See Figure 9.1.)

Figure 9.1
The Concept

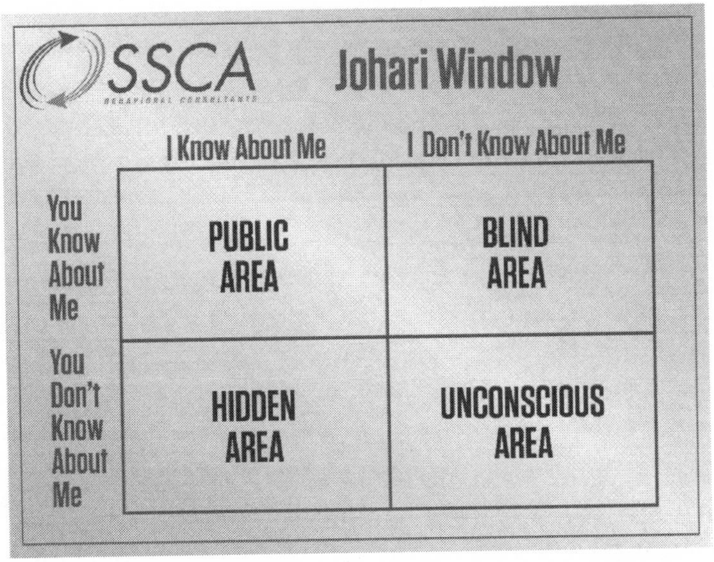

THE PUBLIC AREA: As you can see in Figure 9.1, the area of my personality we both know about is the Public Area, because that is the part of me that we are both aware of. It is an open book to be read by anyone who cares to pick it up. This Public Area is also referred to as the open area, because it reflects aspects of my personality I freely express to others.

THE HIDDEN AREA: The area of my personality that I know about me, but you don't know about me. The Hidden Area is also referred to as the private area because it reflects aspects of my personality I keep to myself. This is called the Hidden Area, because I purposely hide this from others. Usually this is because I believe if you knew these things about me, I would be less acceptable to you. You might even reject me, which would be painful.

THE BLIND AREA: The area of my personality that I don't know about me and you do we call the Blind Area. It comprises things about me I am unaware of and literally do not see in me. And you are often correct in assuming I often don't want to know those things.

THE PRE/UN/SUB CONSCIOUS AREA: The area I don't know about me and you don't know about me is the Unconscious Area. The prefixes *pre, un,* and *sub* reflect varying degrees of conscious area suppression. Despite its relevance for both the sender and receiver of Straight-Line communication, we will spend no time in this brief book on this area, but rather, leave it to you and your Freudian therapist to explore.

In Figure 9.2 (next page), you will see that the areas are drawn in different sizes. This visually portrays the fact that unlike most windowpanes, the sizes of the sections of the Johari Window are not symmetrical. We develop differently, and thus, our Hidden Area may in fact be much larger or much smaller than our Public Area, depending upon who the "you" is in the analysis. The fact is most of us consciously are creating much smaller hidden areas with our best friends and spouses than our bosses and customers. The size of our Blind Area is highly dependent on the social contract we have with others. This social contract provides feedback in the form of leveling, which I will talk about shortly.

Social contracts are stated and unstated agreements between two or more people. Similar to legal contracts, if they're broken, they'll cause tension. But unlike legal contracts, social contracts are not enforceable.

If you're introduced to someone, the rules of the social contract require you to say, "Hi. Nice to meet you," or some other sort of appropriate greeting. If you don't greet someone you're introduced to, you've broken the social contract. The result is tension between you and the other person or group.

Figure 9.2
The Concept in Reality

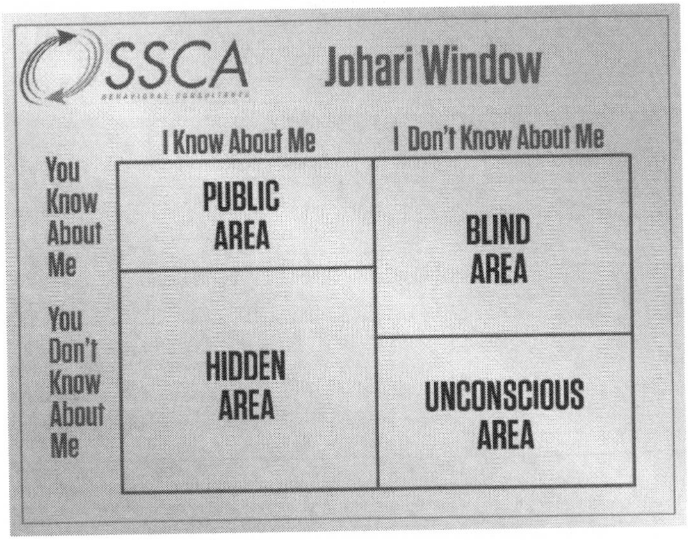

The purpose of bringing this model up, is to point out that I am advocating, that you make the choice to use Straight-Line communication, in order to reduce the size of the Blind Area. When this occurs, aspects about you have moved to your Public Area. Intuitively you know when you are dealing with something from an individual's Blind Area you are walking on thin ice (When I refer to *you* I'm addressing the person and perspective that identifies with "I Know About ME" and "I Don't Know About Me" in the chart).

Leveling and Our Blind Area

The size of our Blind Area is highly dependent on the unspoken social contract we have with others to provide feedback. This feedback comes in the form of leveling, which means you actively seek from others honest feedback. And when you receive it, as hard as it may be, you must resist the temptation to shoot the messenger. Thus, the secret of Straight-Line communication (if you have not figured it out by now) is to create a contract around a helping relationship. At its best, this requires consistent leveling.

Figure 9.3
How to Build the Size of the Public Area

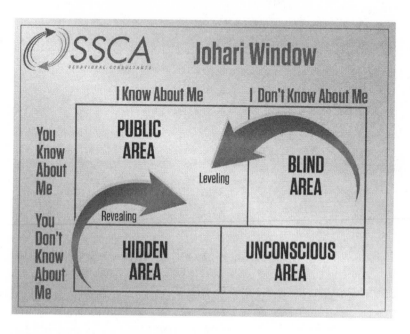

So, in addition to this very practical tool of gaining mastery of actively seeking feedback, in order to become more skilled at Straight-Line communication, you must also use leveling. Leveling is a tool that allows you most effectively to take something out of the Blind Area. Fortunately, a gentleman named Robert Horton outlined guidelines for leveling years ago. Experience tells me when you develop skill in applying these rules, you become much more impactful as a professional helper.

The most productive communication is between people operating from Public Areas. You both know what is going on, and so the context is obvious. When you ask your manager, "What would you think if we ran over budget on this project?" you may be dealing with an unpleasant topic, but your frames of reference are not hidden or unknown.

Reasons for Reducing the Size of Your Hidden Area

Straight-Line communication, when coming from the Hidden Area, is entirely different. Because of its importance, an aside is in order. While we advocate creating as small a Hidden Area as possible for rather obvious reasons, don't ever let anyone tell you that a Hidden Area is not appropriate. Some of your beliefs and inner thoughts are no business of anyone else's, and not sharing them is perfectly healthy. The problem is that most of us create protective mechanisms to hide the person we really are and are paranoid others will find out. Much of our energy is then spent trying to maintain these one-hundred-foot-tall and one-hundred-foot-thick walls. Others then sense this lack of openness and respond in kind. Thus, a curtain of being closed with the associated lack of trust quickly becomes the norm for your relationships.

We often feel vulnerable when we reveal, yet we have much to gain from opening up. We receive what we give out—openness begets openness and closed-ness begets closed-ness. When we are closed, we are inviting others to respond in the same way, and thus, in very subtle ways, lack of vulnerability and openness becomes the norm. I do not need to reveal my deepest, darkest secret to begin to open up a relationship, but not revealing my emotions and reactions leads to mistrust and the need for others to keep themselves defended also. The question is, "Who will open up first?" My recommendation is not to make it a waiting contest.

This also raises the question addressed by the first variable of one of the best-known psychological instruments in the world, called the Myers-Briggs Type Indicator (MBTI). The question is simply, are extroverts more likely to speak their mind than introverts? The answer is no. However, it needs a better explanation. If either type is avoiding being vulnerable, the extravert may volunteer information but may not address the tough issue. If an introvert is asked for their opinion, and is being straight, they will give it, but they are not as likely to initiate the dialogue as an extravert.

Maintaining a large Hidden Area has the impact of isolating us from others, often for no good reason. Ironically, when you finally let down your guard and reveal your most inner fears to a good friend, all too often they look at you quizzically and respond, "Heck, I knew that about you. Heck, everyone knows that." The reality is that items/traits we often think are so well hidden are often out there for all to see, and we are still accepted and acceptable.

It is often when the individual or group we are working with is simply unaware of their behavior or its impact, that Straight-Line communication is most called for and desperately needed. As we stated and illustrated in Figure 9.3, when something is removed from our Blind Area, we call this leveling. Horton maintains it takes a degree of trust between the two parties to have leveling take place.

I would add to Horton's statement that more than trust is needed; a degree of investment in the relationship is a prerequisite. Thus, if you have a dear friend who has a piece of lint on his suit, you are more likely to point it out than if it is a complete stranger or someone you will never see again. I have a strategic partner who had stopped in the men's room just as a cocktail party was beginning following his well-received presentation. His embarrassment was palpable when about a half an hour into the reception someone finally told him that a string of toilet paper was hanging from the back of his pants. Why did not someone tell him earlier?

The consequence of leveling is that it instantaneously moves the item under discussion from the unknown to the known area, which suggests the person has a responsibility now to deal with it. Most of the things in our blind area are either there for a reason or we would really want to know about them. Straight-Line communication is usually targeted at the latter, yet often is most powerful when it makes inroads into the former.

However, just because we want to know if we have a speck of food on our cheek does not mean we are happy to hear it. Most people, even close friends, let you walk around all day with a button undone on your shirt collar, rather than point it out. We have learned from long and hard experience that even the best-intentioned messengers get shot (remember "temporary dislike" in Chapter 7). These examples of innocuous slips by a person pale in comparison to bad breath or hurtful behavior as a topic to be broached.

When you make the choice to level with someone it is usually a risk on your part. Experience tells us that once the reality sets in that you were trying to be helpful and supportive, the relationship changes, and you gain a much more impactful role in the other person's life. Your relationship changes to the point where leveling is the norm and Straight-Line communication is not only expected, but also invited as helpful. You will experience it happening with greater frequency on topics of greater sensitivity. The trust snowballs into a meaningful and helpful energy directed at constant improvement.

Horton's Guidelines

On that note, some of Horton's ground rules for leveling are worthy of review and adoption:

1. **Focus on the behavior rather than the person.** A simple example of this rule would be to tell the person, "Tucking your shirt in will give a more professional appearance and inspire confidence," rather than, "You are a slob; you need to clean up your act."

2. **Focus on observations rather than inferences.** An observation is "you appear tired." An inference is "you are disinterested." An inference is mindreading, your interpretation of what you observe, and an assumption: which may or may not be accurate.

3. **Be descriptive rather than judgmental.** When you report what you observed occur, the response invited is very different from when you evaluate

the behavior. The description is intended and often heard as a much more neutral report. This takes work to become good at, but once mastered, you will experience much less defensiveness from the other person. The reality is that much of judgment is an attack, and when we are attacked, our natural response is to defend. If you think about it, there are biological and psychological responses nature has wisely built into us to preserve the species. An example is, "You arrived ten minutes late for the meeting, and it hurt our ability to use the time effectively," rather than, "Your time priorities are all screwed up, and you obviously don't care."

4. Timing is key. The closer to the behavior the timing of the feedback can take place, the better a chance for learning and minimizing distortion. While you may choose to wait for a private time or to let things cool down, in my experience, Straight-Line communication is best practiced in the here and now. General societal/cultural norms around politeness are often used as an excuse not to confront issues and to allow them to be swept under the rug. Anyone who successfully navigated toilet training with a child learned that the closer to the behavior (both desired and undesired) the feedback is provided, the higher the probability of behavior change.

5. Focus on having the input understood rather than on giving advice. This one is hard. The giving of advice assumes others can use your skills, experience, and frame of reference and the act as you would. Of course, they can't because that background is not relevant to them. The other problem with giving advice is it sometimes is actually asked for, which is tempting to give in to. When it is sought to genuinely grow, offer it freely. But when it is an excuse to shift the responsibility for the outcome onto you, you are being seduced into drama.

6. Focus on the amount of information the person can use, rather than the amount you might like to give. Performing a data dump to be heard is not helpful, because it takes the leveling out of the realm of Straight-Line communication and into the realm of being a frustration release for you. Remember, the goal is to leave the other person helped.

My Additions to Horton's Guidelines

7. Ideally, Straight-Line communication is solicited, not imposed. Often the solicitation is a long-held contract, but just as often it is a quick question, "Could I give you some feedback?" Even when there is a grimace and a begrudging yes, it has escaped from the state of being imposed. This will make a surprising difference in the listening and acceptance of what is being offered for some pretty complex reasons having to do with "power arousal".

8. When Straight-Line communication is given in a group, check for accuracy with others. If they don't agree, it does not mean your impression was necessarily wrong, but provides the insight that your truth might not be their truth. Watch for them saying the same thing in a less confronting manner; many people are extremely uncomfortable with Straight-Line communication and seek to soften your more direct messages. If their input is helpful, welcome it. If it changes the meaning you intended, then provide clarifying information. Always make sure your initial statement was understood the way you meant it to be expressed. With that said, remember that Straight-Line communication is about helping the other person or group grow and become more effective.

The simple recognition that you are taking a piece of information from an individual's Blind Area, and putting it in the Public Area, where it may cause loss of face or otherwise be embarrassing, is a helpful frame of reference. Be aware of this but avoid using it as your sole criteria for avoiding Straight-Line communication. And when applying Straight-Line communication, follow the guidelines for how to do it effectively. By doing so, you can make all the difference as to whether you are truly helpful and take the relationship to a new plane or end up with an embarrassing faux pas you are struggling to overcome.

Learning from Ancient Warriors

Looking back on history, we see the fierce and bloody battles of ancient times. The courage to be in a relatively unorganized large band of men with spears, axes, and swords, facing an equally large band with the same armaments - and then run at them joining in hand-to-hand combat - was the order of the day. Even the smallest of cuts were extremely painful and there were no *M*A*S*H* units with morphine and trained physicians to sterilize the wounds.

The Greeks first developed groundbreaking strategies, which the Romans later adopted and improved upon. Both groups defeated their enemies and expanded their empires by changing the way they went into battle. For example, they developed organizational techniques such as formations, which dramatically improved the way men fought. Think of the courage it took to stand in formation when a force significantly larger than yours was bearing down on you. This was what they often faced when fighting their rivals. The change in tactics and strategy required acceptance of a new approach, practice, and discipline, which led them to success. This is fundamentally the shift we need to make when we adopt a new approach to our communications pattern.

The Greeks and Romans did not just find a way to improve individual soldiers' skills with a sword, but also redesigned its length and how it was used in close quarters. In business, we call this process improvement. History reveals that a foe using a traditional approach—even with dramatically superior numbers—in battle against the skilled, well-trained, and disciplined Roman army, was doomed to lose. The fact was, however, that first attempts in using the new methods in war took a great deal of courage. The same is true of using Straight-Line communication.

Changing Your Modus Operandi

A more contemporary example of people and systems adopting change comes from a book written by two very influential army generals, Gordon Sullivan and Michael Harper, *Hope Is Not a Method: What Business Leaders Can Learn from America's Army* (Broadway Books, 1996). They point out the changes in approach used in the world of high jumping in the last century.

In Figure 9.4 (next page), you will see four distinctly different approaches to running up to and then hurdling your body over a bar. This is a contest with one goal: to see how high you can get without knocking the bar off its precarious perch. Remember, this is not the pole vault, so there has been no improvement in technology. While we may have gotten a bit stronger and faster, there are no new plastics or other artificial, external factors.

Figure 9.4

High Jump Data

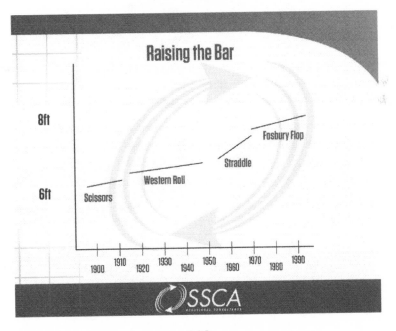

As you can see, a mediocre Western roll jumper would easily beat the world record holder using the scissor kick approach, and so it is with the progression to the straddle and then the Fosbury Flop. But how would you like to be a pioneer of the new, relatively unproven and awkward techniques?

The courage to attempt a new approach, and then train long enough to perfect it, keeps most of us from even attempting. And indeed, that is where we are with Straight-Line communication. At some point, we will be better at it because we will have practiced hard and developed the skills, not because of any moral preaching, but rather, because in this competitive world we must do so to be a world-class executive. And we do this despite the fact anything new is difficult and feels and looks awkward when we first attempt it.

This is a difficult-to-measure fundamental process change that, when adopted, will create a competitive advantage over those who are unaware of it or choose not to adopt it. Again, I refer you to the chapter titled, "What It Ain't" (Chapter 3), because simple and small errors in approach are the difference between being lost in the crowd of also-rans, and world-class performance.

Don't be afraid to seek help in perfecting your technique. As my son once pointed out to me, the only people without coaches are amateurs not trying to get better. Every professional athlete of merit, from the best football players to the best tennis and golf professionals, actively seeks coaching to continue to improve his or her game. I would offer one note of caution: if you hire the best scissors-technique coach who trained the Olympic Games winner in 1912, you will be behind the competition. No matter how qualified and caring he or she is, if you want to be the best in class, you must use best current practices, regardless how difficult it is to adopt them.

Gladwell: How New Ideas Catch On

It is pretty obvious why the new high jump technique gained in popularity so quickly. Clearly a different technique that gets superior results cannot be ignored by competitors. And so, for Straight-Line communication—how long will it take for other organizations to adopt the new norms of Straight-Line communication, when you are the only one initially practicing the approach?

As it turns out, it may not take as long as you think. The question of spreading a concept like this was addressed in Malcolm Gladwell's first book, *The Tipping Point: How Little Things Can Make a Big Difference* (Little, Brown and Company, 2000). While not a researcher or even practitioner in the field, he is an excellent writer who outlines the process by which ideas catch hold in society, and how it takes a ridiculously small group to advance the concept.

Gladwell describes that contagious behavior is catchy in a very predictable manner. The first step is you need a carrier of the new idea because he or she wants to. No other reason is needed. The second is that very small acts have very large consequences. Thus, it will be the simple things that are almost unnoticeable by themselves that will add up to a big shift. And third, the change in the systematic behavior will happen very rapidly, not gradually. The rise will be very much like an epidemic, and then it simply needs to be nurtured.

To apply Gladwell's steps to Straight-Line communication, we need a carrier of the idea who will start using this technique. Next, the impact of Straight-Line communication will begin in a few businesses that interact with that one. Then, we will see the major impact as Straight-Line communication takes hold and spreads.

Moore's Steps for Technological Implementation

Perhaps the best student of this is Dr. Geoffrey Moore, whose first book, *Crossing the Chasm: Marketing and Selling Disruptive Products to Mainstream Customers* (Harper Business, 2014), looks at the factors involved in bringing a new high-tech product to market. Admittedly, a new behavior pattern is not a high-tech product, but perhaps we can learn something from Moore about the process of adoption, that goes a bit beyond Gladwell's insights.

As a business man, I particularly like Dr. Moore's approach, as it looks at the problem from a segmented market perspective. He maintains the adoption process has four unique markets, that each has very different drivers, which cause them to purchase a new product during a product's life cycle.

Figure 9.5
Product Adoption Cycle

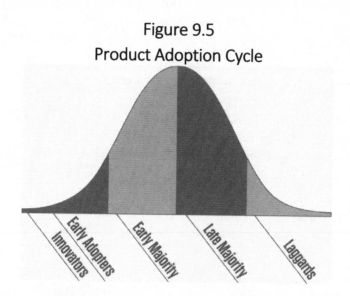

Bell curve of technology implementation. Source: *Crossing the Chasm*, Geoffrey A. Moore, Harper Business Publishing, 1991 (p. 12).

According to Moore, as shown in Figure 9.5, the Early Adopters—relatively few in number—are willing to try something out in its early stages and tinker with it to make it work. They do not need proof the concept works but, rather, can envision a utility and therefore see its possibilities. Despite the early setbacks associated with every beta site and unproven product, they will stick with it while it is being perfected. Each and every early product, from cell phones to laptops to UBER, you would not live without today, was at one time no joy at all. If the early adopters had not been there to fiddle and improve it, these innovations would not have made it in the market. And the truth is, the early adopters went through pain attempting to make the product perform.

Regardless of merit, products that succeed are seldom the ones that were initially introduced.

The Early Majority are greater in number than the Early Adopters. They accept the new technology when trusted references who have adopted the product speak to its reliability, and attest to the fact that it meets its promises (Moore's book is about how most products fall into a chasm between these two groups and how to avoid that painful death). The problem for businesses introducing a new product occurs when it lacks sufficient expert support to induce the Early Majority to purchase it.

Next to accept the product is the Late Majority. This very large market segment will only purchase (or in this case adopt an idea) once it is proven. They will not be close to adopting something that has risk involved, but by this time, it is a proven concept. Since everyone else is on the bandwagon, it is time for them to join.

The last segment is referred to as Laggards. This is a market segment we should forget about putting much time or energy into changing. When and if they adopt our concept, it will be almost by mistake. Because it is a norm that caught on years ago, they may now purchase a basic cell phone (horrors if it texts).

Where Do You Fit in this Cycle?

If you look at the diagram closely, you will notice I left out discussing a very thin sliver of the marketplace. They come before the Early Adopters and are referred to as Innovators. They are truly few and far between. When speaking of a product, this unique psychographic group is different in many respects. First, they are technology geeks who will figure out how to use the black box. Second, they are often crusaders who want badly to birth the new concept. They become passionate about making it work. When it comes to Straight-Line communication, you'll be somewhere along this curve either by choice or happenstance. I suggest you opt for choice.

While there are few innovators, they are extremely important. That is where you may come in if you are one of the early readers of this book. For instance, the way to get ideas accepted, according to politicians (who are the experts in this field), is through education.

By using Straight-Line communication to educate those around you, over time, they'll see how it increases efficiency, decreases confusion, and improves how the entire organization runs.

Making this type of macro-level change, however, requires a commitment on your part to postponing gratification. Those around you may not realize the benefit of Straight-Line communication right away. But, as I've seen over and over again throughout my consulting career, its merits will eventually come through. And when your colleagues see the power of Straight-Line communication, they'll recognize the importance of making it a part of how they work with you.

Thus, if you choose to be an innovator in this concept, you are also becoming an educator, usually by your role modeling rather than preaching. You will initially be viewed as a bit of a geek but returning to the lessons of Gladwell's *The Tipping Point*, the small changes will add up, and one day, just as with your ubiquitous smart phone, you will look back and have a hard time remembering when you were comfortable leaving home without this tool.

A very good reason this how-to chapter does not need to be too long is there are a many extremely good books on related topics. Although they don't focus on Straight-Line communication with the single-minded laser of this work, they do give keys for how to word your conversations.

The book, *Crucial Conversations: Tools for Talking When Stakes Are High* by Kerry Patterson, Joseph Grenny, Ron McMillan, and Al Switzler (McGraw-Hill, 2002) gives an excellent step-by-step insight in how to handle the conversations that are "defining moments in our lives."

On page twenty-three of chapter two, they say, "At the core of every successful conversation lies the free flow of relevant information. People openly and honestly express their opinions, share their feelings, and articulate their theories. They willingly and capably express their views, *even when their ideas are controversial or unpopular.*" While I am talking about many more conversations than those that are defining moments, the guidelines the authors give are very useful when using Straight-Line communication. Those interested in becoming masters of Straight-Line communication will want to read this how-to manual.

By definition, people who avoid "crucial conversations" are in quadrant 3 and 4 (see matrix from Chapter 5: "The Message or the Messenger?" below).

Figure 5.1
Message Content Versus Delivery

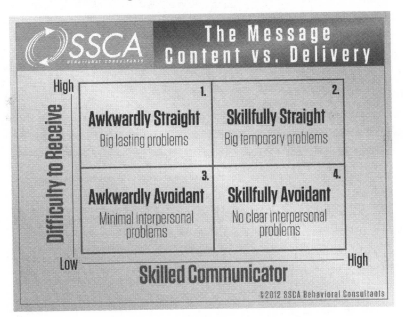

The Straight-Line

The reality is that we can all improve our communications skills and abilities. There is an entire industry that has thrived over the years on improving the effectiveness of those determined to get better at driving change, communicating, and motivating. At its essence, this is what great leaders do, and most were not born with the skills they now possess.

It does not take rocket science to recognize that since WWII, when modern management and leadership development got its start, the emphasis has been on the horizontal axis - that is developing how we deliver the message - not what we speak about. The developmental models have emphasized delivering the messages so they can be heard, understood, and acted upon with grace. I have no problem with this, and as a matter of fact, think it is extremely important.

The problem is that there has not been an equal emphasis on speaking out honestly. Put simply, we have consciously and systematically developed the ability to know when we are feeling vulnerable, and be trained to act accordingly, not just on automatic pilot. Thus, we get messages delivered effectively and with high impact. And at the same time, we have ignored the content of what is being brought to the table. The race to continue our development at becoming skilled is far from over. The resulting problem: we are living in the lower quadrants (with the inability to speak honestly) as highly effective communicators, immersed in great discussions that are off target - and therefore we won't make much of a difference.

You can get better at Straight-Line communication. But I must warn you, the journey to becoming a great leader is a marathon without a finish line. It is a run you will never finish, but the effort will pay off in spades. And you will find that, increasingly, Straight-Line communication will be one of the requisite tools and tactics in your success.

One more thing is necessary. I saw it put best on the whiteboard in the quarterback coaching room of the University of Syracuse football team. I walked in on the quarterback coach while he was reviewing game film with the QBs. On the whiteboard in bold letters was the phrase, "Be where your ass is!" I had to see if it meant what I thought, so before I left, I asked for an explanation from the coach. He turned to one of the tall, athletic young men in the room and said, "Why don't you explain it."

The young man looked at me and with no hesitation explained, "If you are in class be in class; don't be daydreaming about your girlfriend. If you are at practice, be at practice; don't be worried about your test the next day." Speaking for myself, this is a far more powerful way to express what we often advocate as being in the moment or being present.

In order to really convey my complete experience, despite the fact I may feel vulnerable, I need to "be where my ass is" so I am actually aware of the experience. This is possible only if I am paying attention, and then move the pre/subconscious thought to the conscious part of my thinking. I can then examine it and make the decision in the light of day as to whether I will express it or not.

When you are reading this book are you really here? Your ass is, so why not invite your brain?

Ed Monser's Practical Input:

My dreaded task

One of the most unpleasant and challenging tasks for any business leader is to make the decision to close an operation. There is no doubt as the global economy continues to evolve and new technologies change the markets, shutdowns and closures will always be with us. They always have and I do not know any executive who does not lose sleep over these disrupting decisions.

I have been directly involved in the closure of a number of facilities over the years and have consistently been struck with the power of Straight-Line communications as both a key to helping the individuals impacted and the company maintain its commitments. From the Johari window the key is leveling with people, minimizing the blind area and the hidden area, and maximizing the public area. Once the decision has been made, the fewer the secrets the better. The more information you get into the Public area, the better. All this is of course easy to say but takes a great deal of courage to do.

After the business case has been made and confirmed that an operation needs to be closed, the communications plan to all involved needs to be put together. There is always a debate on when people should be told. One line of thinking is to wait as long as possible before public announcements come out. The argument is usually that you want to minimize disruptions till inventories are built to cover any needs for the transition. When this option is picked, you are not using Straight-Line communications. Interestingly the results are usually much more disruption and problems come with the delay. Many times, there is a leak of information that then causes many questions that drive to a loss of trust, and an ultimate destruction of all productivity.

I have come to firmly believe the best option is after the decision has been made, be straight with your people. Answer the questions they have. And amazingly, since you are likely communicating more and more directly than before the closure announcement, trust goes up at the operations, and quality and productivity improves as the shut-down activities take place. Once you tell your employees what their benefits are, what are the severance package details, what are their recall rights, that references will be provided along with help in finding alternate employment, and given in writing how each person is going to be treated, people almost always choose to do their job, and many choose to do it better than any time before the announcement of closure. After reviewing the performance for the last group of plants we have closed, each were notified six months before closure, the improved performance was dramatic. The plant improved on-time delivery, inventory turnover, cash generation, profitability, safety performance, quality performance, and lowered employee turnover during the final twelve months of operation.

Horton's guidelines for leveling are very helpful in how to communicate, how to be straightforward, with this difficult communication. Focus on the behavior and not the person, focus on observations rather than inferences, being descriptive rather than judgmental, focus on having input understood, focus on information the person can use, and be sure to follow-up and check for understanding with all involved. It is fine to announce things to the group, but individual, one-on-one communications are needed.

My clear preference when a plant closure is the only option is to announce as soon as the decision is final and you have your plan in place, including a well thought out communications plan. Follow the Horton guidelines on leveling and give the people the information they need. With all this, announcements as much as year before closure can and do work. Being straight with your people is the absolute key. And despite the fact that it is part of the job our executive team must do, I can say without fear of contradiction, it is the least favorite and we all lose sleep wondering what we did wrong to have to make these painful calls that impact individuals and entire communities.

The Straight-Line

Chapter 10

Your Compass

"Faced with the choice between changing one's mind and proving there is no need to do so, almost everyone gets busy on the proof."

-John Kenneth Galbraith

One of the great movies of the past decade that is being discovered by a new generation is *Scent of a Woman*. At the end of the movie, there is an unforgettable confrontation between Colonel Slade, played by Al Pacino, and the strict headmaster of a traditional East Coast boarding school. (If you haven't seen this classic, it is worth renting!) They are in front of the assembled students and faculty to determine the fate of Charlie, a schoolboy who witnessed the perpetrators of a school prank (blown way out of proportion), but who refuses to reveal their names. Colonel Slade sits next to Charlie while the headmaster vilifies Charlie for not identifying his classmates.

Making the Hard Decision

There is much more intrigue to the scene, which would justify Charlie throwing the guilty three elitist turkeys, who are in the audience, under the bus. To take the courageous position not to name names is to put his future at great peril, as he has been threatened with disgrace and expulsion for non-cooperation. Another witness has folded, but that boy's evidence is "not verifiable" because his powerful alumni father is sitting ominously by his side as a protector. Only after it becomes clear Charlie has made the decision not to give in does Colonel Slade come to his aid. At one point in a brilliantly written monologue he makes a very compelling point. He states, "I don't know if Charlie's silence here today is right or wrong. I am not a judge or jury. But I can tell you this: he won't sell anybody out to buy his future! And that, my friends, is called courage; it's called integrity. Now that's the stuff leaders should be made of...Now I have come to the crossroads in my life ... I always knew what the right path was; without exception I knew. But I never took it...You know why? ... Because it was TOO DAMN HARD!!"

What he was saying was clear: I know the direction of true north. I have an inner compass. I am not lost. I know the road to take.

Make no mistake—so do you. When it comes to knowing when and whether to be forthright, there is seldom any doubt.

I am not often confronted with the question of what Straight-Line communication is in any given situation. And neither are you. The issue is not uncertainty of the right road to take, but whether it is "too damn hard." We seldom blatantly lie but, instead, leave a part of the dialogue unstated. We don't tell the whole truth, which means we are participating in a psychological game.

Exposing Our Vulnerability

The richness of the movie scene reveals another interesting facet of using Straight-Line communication. Colonel Slade made a crucial decision: to be vulnerable. He made a statement most of us can identify with. The embarrassing admission of this proud soldier—that he always knew the right road but didn't have the courage to follow his convictions—is one most of us can relate to but prefer to keep to ourselves. Being that vulnerable in front of strangers and, even more difficult, in front of friends, or an audience you would like to think highly of you, is hard. Using Straight-Line communication more often than not requires a degree of vulnerability, which can feel uncomfortable at best and terrifying at worst.

I purposely call out vulnerability separately, rather than leaving it lumped with my discussion of fears, under whose umbrella it justifiably finds a home. This is because it is so easy to recognize when it occurs. The simple act of showing vulnerability holds a unique potency in placing the exposed individual in one of two extremes—(1) deepened respect because the person is willing to step over this fear; and (2) truthfully share his or her humanity and risk complete rejection, because he or she is an unworthy soul whose revelation has so alienated us that further contact is painful.

I hypothesize true vulnerability evokes such a strong response in us because people so rarely expose themselves in this way. If it happened every day, we would be anesthetized to its effects, and its power would be diminished.

James "Jamie" Dimon, the CEO of JPMorgan Chase, demonstrated the power of such vulnerability, at a business school graduation ceremony I attended. He made a good speech, as graduation addresses go, and it went beyond the usual platitudes about how to live your life. It was an honor that this role model returned to his alma mater to speak with these aspiring business leaders, who could only hope for his level of success.

Fearless Sharing Begins with Self-honesty

We were not at all surprised to hear Jamie Dimon tell the graduates that their lives would be a series of ups and downs. However, I can recall only one specific story from his talk, and the memory comes back to me viscerally. Dimon revealed that the very public announcement of his departure from Smith Barney "to pursue other interests and for personal reasons" was face-saving bunk. "The fact is Sandy Weil fired me." You could have heard a pin drop in the audience of thousands. He spoke of the embarrassment and pain in telling his wife and family and of how hard that time was for him. The audience was in disbelief as this "captain of the industry," a wealthy and highly successful executive, went on to speak of the struggles during the next year in finding a new position and some of the personal doubts he had to work through.

The Straight-Line

The revelation was not a punch line to impress but rather an essential point to help others with their inevitable struggles, which is essentially what a graduation speaker is asked to do. Most fail to deliver. Too often, they are attempting to become the role model they believe is the reason they were selected for the honor in the first place.

And each person there, most of all the honored speakers themselves, know the painting is in part distorted if not an outright lie. Richard Feynman, the late Nobel winning physicist in a rather irreverent look back over his life, *Surely, You're Joking, Mr. Feynman! Adventures of a Curious Character* (W. W. Norton & Company, 1997) said it best, "The first principle is that you must not fool yourself and you are the easiest person to fool."

Because Dimon decided to take the road of vulnerability, he created a potent bond based on his humanity. I, for one, did not dwell on the flaws that led to his being fired but rather the remarkable fact that he was admitting to it in front of an audience he wanted to hold him in high regard. He did not try to justify his behavior or demean Sandy Weil but, rather, shared that even those at the top of the pyramid have painful setbacks they would prefer to hide on the journey. And while it may not be a case for celebration, there is little shame in it.

And he expressed it with genuine humility—or so it seemed to me, and I hope it was. I often find that vulnerability is mislabeled or judged to come automatically packaged with humility. They are very different. And while often vulnerability encompasses humility, humility and vulnerability often do not come as a package deal. It is a lesson well thought through on the way to Straight-Line communication.

Ed Monser's Practical Input:

You're Going to Get Fired

My father looked right at me and said, "You're going to be fired." He said this from his hospital bed, where he lay dying. My father was fifty-three years old, his body and brain shutting down from terminal illness. I was thirty years old at the time, working at my first big job after finishing my engineering degree and spending my weekends at my father's bedside in a Chicago hospital. On these weekends, I would sit quietly while he slept, waiting for the fleeting moments of conversation we would grab before he would drift back off. But while our conversations were brief, they were remarkable for their candor, in fact, sometimes alarmingly so— for example I'd never really wanted to know the story surrounding my own conception, but I got it nevertheless.

"You're going to be fired," he repeated.

"It's the weekend, Dad, don't worry," I responded, thinking he was concerned that I was taking time off to be with him. "That's not what I meant," he said. "I know you. At some point, I know you're going to be fired. Myself? I was fired three times." This came as a complete surprise to me. Growing up, I was aware that my father had been laid off or changed jobs but never that he had been fired from any position he had held.

"One time was for bad timing. One time was for bad luck. And one time was because I did something wrong."

I listened attentively as he exposed a part of his professional life I knew nothing about.

"The first time I was fired was because I was in the wrong place at the wrong time. It was at an office Christmas party. I ducked back into my office to grab something before leaving and caught my boss in a compromising position with

129

a coworker. The very next day I was called into his office and fired. The second time, my company was taken over by a larger corporation. The merger created two of everything, and suddenly I was redundant. I got the axe.

"But the third time...the third time was because I did something wrong. I made a big mistake. I changed the numbers on a report so my team's performance would look better and we would get paid more. It was discovered; I was fired.

"I can tell you quite clearly, lying here dying, knowing what I know, that the first two times do not bother me in the least. But to this day, I cannot stop thinking about that third time when I did something wrong. I still feel bad about it. Trust me. You do not want to end your life as I am with a failure like this hanging over your head. I know how important it is for you to do well and achieve your goals, and I know you will be tempted to do things to enhance your position. I know you're going to make mistakes, and I know you're going to be fired. Just make sure you're fired for doing the right thing." The conversation ended here, and he drifted back off into sleep.

I was stunned. Many thoughts were racing through my brain. Why had all this been hidden from me for so long? Why did it take so long for my father and me to have a straightforward conversation like this? Why had he felt so vulnerable, and fearful, and why did he see the need to have me see him in a certain contrived way? Why did he feel safer now and was willing to share and teach? At the time I knew this was a very memorable conversation. This dramatically changed our relationship, and there was closeness between us that had been missing for a very long time. And I could not anticipate how many times I would hear my father's words come back to me throughout my career? I hear them still with no less frequency several times a week.

And could I have anticipated how many times opportunities would arise where I could have easily decided to make the wrong choice? A choice to inflate, or to change, or to alter or to enhance? These choices are available to all of us every day; they are certainly tempting. I've faced such choices innumerable times in my career, and I consider myself lucky to have my father's voice helping me.

Maybe even more important was the idea of sharing my vulnerability with my own children. Every time I have taken the risk of opening up with my children I have been rewarded with closeness and love that we all crave and need.

His words are a terrific compass in the storm; they have helped me draw a straight, firm line in the sand. Using Straight-Line communication with others is imperative but using Straight-Line communication with yourself can often be the more difficult task.

The Straight-Line

Chapter 11

In Case You Need a Reason—Some Research

"Silence is an argument carried out by other means."

-Ernesto "Che" Guevara

Jim Collins is a serious researcher. His books *Built to Last: Successful Habits of Visionary Companies* (with Jerry Porras) (HarperCollins, 1994), and *Good to Great* (HarperCollins, 2001) have appendices as long as the hearts of many popular management books. I am a pushover to buy whatever he prints because of his rigor and discipline. My quest for statistical proof is so intense that my wife maintains I was an engineer in a former life. (I don't believe it because there is no proof of former lives and, yes, she has to live with me). Our clients don't often hear "trust me on this" from us because we have such a strong research bias.

Collins's least known book is titled, *How the Mighty Fall And Why Some Companies Never Give In* (HarperCollins, 2009), and is a critical examination of what leads to the downfall of the world's great corporations - and why some avoid death (this is a short book with a total of 227 pages—of which 95 are appendices: as I said, he is my hero).

While the book is worth reading for those interested in the topic, pages 77 and 78 are particularly powerful. In a small piece of the book entitled "A Culture of Denial," he presents one of the most compelling arguments for Straight-Line communication I have seen yet. It is a simple chart with only two columns. Yet, how managers interact says a lot about the state of the company.

The Straight-Line

According to Jim Collins in his book, *How the Mighty Fall and Why Some Companies Never Give In,* he lists 8 patterns of executive team behavior that occur when the company is either starting to fail or, is on its way to doing well. Number one on the list for a team "on their way down," is that "people shield those in power from unpleasant facts, fearful of penalties and criticism for shining light on the rough realities". When looking at the behavior of patterns of executive teams when companies are performing very well, the first item he lists is, "people bring forth grim facts— 'Come here and look, man, this is ugly' —to be discussed; leaders never criticize those who bring forth harsh realities in each case". Dr. Collin's work is well worth reading— this is his least known book that is a very powerful piece of research.

I can tell you this chart was not put together on a hunch. The background data gathering and even the wording was agonized over. If I am not mistaken, what they say in in the first entries in each column in this chart is companies that grow and thrive use Straight-Line communication, and companies that waste away their once great position do not. I was not there, but I can't help but think the reason this was listed as the first of the eight points was not a random act.

When I share this with executives, they look at me as if to say, "Of course, we know that." And then they go on running their meetings with only a benign attempt at ensuring the rules of engagement look like those of teams in thriving corporations.

And from a much less rigorous piece, yet still a book with much wisdom, comes another list. Dr. David Maister was a Harvard Business School professor who specialized in the professional service firms. In his work through the years, he drew many conclusions about what made the "great ones" great and the "also-rans" not so great. His early work culminated in two books, *Managing the Professional Service Firm* and *True Professionalism,* and were rife with the statistics to back up his conclusions.

134

The Trusted Advisor

His latest work with Charles Green and Robert Galford, *The Trusted Advisor* (Touchstone, 2001), is not so rigorous, and is based much more on the accumulation of experience. This book is a bible for any serious consultant, from lawyer to accountant. While his focus is on the Trust Equation (by now you must realize I love formulas and equations), that is not the reason I bring up this body of knowledge. Almost lost, early on (cited on page four and not referred to again) is a twenty-two-item listing of the criteria for the trusted advisor. It is brilliant in both its succinct covering of the waterfront and what they have chosen to leave out.

He lists 22 attributes of high-performing people in the service industry. The whole book is very interesting and one I recommend, and in particular, numbers 9, 10, and 14 on the list are the essential variables of Straight-Line communication.

Here is a listing of traits that our trusted advisors have in common. They:

1. Seem to understand us, effortlessly, and like us
2. Are consistent (we can depend on them)
3. Always help us see things from fresh perspectives
4. Don't try to force things on us
5. Help us think things through (it's our decision)
6. Don't substitute their judgment for ours
7. Don't panic or get overemotional (they stay calm)
8. Help us think and separate our logic from our emotion
9. **Criticize and correct us gently, lovingly**
10. **Don't pull their punches (we can rely on them to tell us the truth)**
11. Are in it for the long haul (the relationship is more important than the current issue)
12. Give us reasoning (to help us think), not just their conclusions
13. Give us options, increase our understanding of those options, give us their recommendation, and let us choose

14. **Challenge our assumptions (help us uncover the false assumptions we've been working under)**
15. Make us feel comfortable and casual personally (but they take the issues seriously)
16. Act like a real person, not someone in a role
17. Are reliably on our side and always seem to have our interests at heart
18. Remember everything we ever said (without notes)
19. Are always honorable (they don't gossip about others, and we trust their values)
20. Help us put our issues in context, often through the use of metaphors, stories, and anecdotes (few problems are completely unique)
21. Have a sense of humor to diffuse (our) tension in tough situations
22. Are smart (sometimes in ways we're not)

As it turns out, the authors have discovered over their years of consulting to the giants in the field (the cover has a testimony from the CEO of the Boston Consulting Group) that being honest is a necessary component to being a highly paid advisor. Again, when I share this with people trying to break into my field, they stand and salute. And when they admit failure and are looking for a job inside a company because they could not make a living as a consultant, a thorough and exhaustive debrief reveals they tried to please rather than risk losing a client by risking Straight-Line communication. The fact is the executives high enough on the food chain to command the budgets to hire us know the difference and don't pay to be patronized for long.

The ability and willingness to use Straight-Line communication is the prerequisite for success in many fields. Therefore, those with greater competency at it will do far better in the long run. Fortunately, those without the natural ability can develop this skill. And both groups—those who naturally use Straight-Line communication and those who must learn it—need to constantly sharpen the saw, to paraphrase Stephen Covey.

Ed Monser's Practical Input:

A Comment

I want to say Amen to Brad's comments on the need for consultants to be straight in order to be effective. The same thing is clearly true in business. It still surprises me how many times seemingly nice consultants fail because they cannot use Straight-Line communications. Their inability to level with others, to choose Straight-Line communication, led to their losing us as a customer.

The Straight-Line

Chapter 12

In Case You Still Need Another Reason—Life's Little Regrets

"If you can find a path with no obstacles, it probably doesn't lead anywhere."

-Frank A. Clark

In a piece by Bonnie Ware, a nurse who worked in palliative care (she shared the last three to twelve weeks of people's lives), she spoke to the regrets they expressed. She lumped the regrets into five categories. Number three was simple: "I wish I'd had the courage to express my feelings."

She goes on to editorialize: "Many people suppressed their feelings in order to keep peace with others. As a result, they settled for a mediocre existence and never became who they were truly capable of becoming. Many developed illnesses relating to the bitterness and resentment they carried as a result.

We cannot control the reactions of others. However, although people may initially react when you change the way you are by speaking honestly, in the end it raises the relationship to a whole new and healthier level. Either that or it releases the unhealthy relationship from your life. Either way, you win." (Ware, 2012).

This was the conclusion of folks who were about to die. We see instances of this all the time among the living.

"I can't believe I didn't speak up at the time! I am so stupid! If only I had not kept my mouth shut..." and he went on venting for about fifteen minutes about several occasions at the office he wanted to take back. This meeting took place at a Starbucks about a year ago. I was sitting across from a very dejected senior vice president of marketing, who was about to resign under pressure, and who was knee deep in his own blood because of the punishment he was bestowing upon himself. The pain he was experiencing was palpable.

It is one of the numerous examples that come to mind when I have been involved in an "end of role" (a little more forgiving than the end of life) discussion. The reality is it is extremely painful. The major distinction between this and what the nurse described, is that you will have the opportunity to address the issue and deal with it differently in your next position. But will you?

*All five are:

1. I wish I had had the courage to live life true to myself, not the life others expected of me.
2. I wish I didn't work so hard.
3. I wish I'd had the courage to express my feelings.
4. I wish I had stayed in touch with my friends.
5. I wish that I had let myself be happier.

Chapter 13

Conclusion

"An invasion of armies can be resisted, but not an idea whose time has come."

-Victor Hugo

We have reviewed the rationale for why each of us is better off individually and collectively when we practice the art of Straight-Line communication. We have reviewed the more obvious reasons we don't use it but should, as well as sometimes when it is appropriate to refrain from using it. We have even talked about sometimes when we don't think it is entirely appropriate.

And we have discussed why using Straight-Line communication feels so unnatural and, thus, is so hard to apply. The practicalities of child rearing, fear, and even biology weigh heavily against it. So, is there hope?

It turns out sociologists (they study group behavior as opposed to psychologist who study individual behavior) would say yes, because society's norms are ever shifting. While we are usually not conscious of practices and beliefs we as a society hold, they are very powerful and dictate much of what we do and think. This includes changes in our behavior that occur without much notice day to day. Political scientists study these subtle shifts carefully, as they dictate who is elected and reflect the changing values in a culture.

Sociologists describe normative behavior as what we, as members of a group within society, "do" - sometimes with unspoken agreement. Examples are as simple as what people consider acceptable dress in various situations. And, like all society's norms, these are open to change. Not long ago, a private country club, much to the delight of many members and chagrin of others, changed the dress code so that men can now eat in the dining room without

141

a sports coat. This controversial breakthrough came in the year 2012. They are pending implementation of the novel idea of allowing "dressy" jeans at the club. Of course, men must still wear a collared shirt to tee off, but everyone seems to accept this as the only proper golf attire that gentlemen wear when chasing their dreams of a par.

This club was not the first to adopt the new dress code, and in fact, is probably a laggard in this regard. Interestingly, the fact that most others had already done so made it possible. Sociologists point to a phenomenon they refer to as "contagious behavior" as influencing individuals' decisions to change. The layman's term is "herd mentality." It is more acceptable to behave in a certain manner and follow written and unwritten rules when your peers are doing so.

Simultaneously, another force was exerting pressure on this prestigious club. The recession had hit golf-club memberships hard, and the board of directors found itself in the uneasy position of not having a waiting list of outsiders wanting to purchase the memberships of those seeking to sell. A survey revealed the potential young marketplace found the "jacket only" policy out of date, and a negative they did not have to put up with, as the competitive clubs had abolished it. Economists refer to this as "competitive advantage" in a free marketplace.

As organizations develop, the Darwinian principles will, as they always have, prevail. Darwin is commonly said to have stated, "Only the strong survive." Thus, the slowest of the herd of buffalo are caught and killed leaving the strongest males and females to pass on a gene pool of stronger and swifter buffalo.

This is not only misquoted but badly misrepresented. What was actually said is, "It is not the strongest of the species that survives, nor the most intelligent, but rather the one most responsive to change." It appears there is a misattribution on this also. In fact, the quote is prominently placed in the stone floor of the headquarters of the California Academy of Sciences, but Darwin's name has been removed as the source of it.

What we will see over time is the organizations and relationships that grow and flourish will do so by responding and changing. And predictably, one of the adaptations necessitated by our age of technology is a norm of greater speed. As we have discussed, the single largest barrier to speed in decision-making and implementation is failure to use Straight-Line communication.

Thus, organizations that exceed others at adopting this behavior as a norm will gain a clear competitive advantage. And when this occurs, the herd mentality, which has valued politeness at the expense of Straight-Line communication, will maintain politeness but swiftly move to punish both the individuals and the organizations that refuse to adapt to the more successful behavior.

A new definition of work effectiveness will become the norm. The old definition of "nice" as proper behavior will be discarded. That "nice" results in layoffs because we allow the company down the street or across the ocean to take our market due to not adopting straight line communication will rapidly change. If we don't respond, we will all be dinosaurs.

A couple of other forces are at play in our world today, whether we like it or not. My great-grandparents grew up with the swiftest form of communication, the telegraph, a vast improvement over the Pony Express. This was unforeseen and unimaginable to those with horses and carriages who lit their houses with lanterns. This new technology dominated for years, and the newspaper was able to bring news of a Civil War battle to your door in Bennington, Vermont, in a matter of days. But even with this increased speed, the questions you had about the fight would have to wait or never be answered.

The Straight-Line

My great-grandparents were amazed with the next advancement in communication—the introduction of the radio, which became the norm for the next generation, my grandparents.

This medium once again had a major impact on the speed and completeness of communications and allowed for a huge new industry of entertainment to take root. The norms and mores of a society quickly shifted. At about the same time, crude telephones made two-way communications possible, and you could quickly get an answer to a burning question if you reached the right person.

The impossible occurred when the radio was replaced by the television for our parents, and once again the complexity, completeness, and dispersal of information took a huge leap. Talk about shifts in societal norms and contagious behavior changes! The TV program *American Bandstand* changed what music in the form of vinyl records was bought, how long the songs were popular, and what clothes were worn.

The advent of the personal computer looked innocent enough by comparison—just a combination typewriter and TV screen. My generation grew up on that medium, and the transformation was far from so simple. The quantity of information at our fingertips and the demands of work suddenly changed with the advent of email and attachments.

This has given way to the Google, Facebook, LinkedIn, and other connections over the Internet for my son's generation. And the resulting change in immediate feedback has led (and will continue to lead) to the expectation for even more speed in day-to-day processes, and the tolerance for far less patience. For this generation, especially, this affects everything from customer service to restaurant reservations. No longer do students go to a library or the massive volumes of the *Encyclopedia Britannica*, books my parents proudly sacrificed to buy for our home-reference library. Google has the answers, immediately. And if the speed of the connection slows down, there is hell to pay.

This is a force of no small impact, and employers ignore it at their peril. As we have said, in business, the one major remaining barrier to this increased speed in decision making and problem solving is lack of candor.

There is another force many in my generation find disturbing in our sons and daughters, that is being noted by students of both psychology and sociology. I am referring to the trend toward a greater willingness to be open and share publicly things we simply did not have the technology to share. More than that, even if we could have told the world, we would not have because the norms of the times would have resulted in embarrassment at the least, and outcast at the worst. Thus, a party occurs on Friday, and virtually simultaneously, Twitters' tweets and pictures are voluntarily (usually) transmitted to a community, which is enlarged by a magnitude as unimaginable to my parents as an airplane would have been to George Washington.

And then we must layer on top of that the demand for transparency, which is difficult to object to by most business people (what are you trying to hide and why?). With Wikipedia publishing even the top secrets of the CIA, we find this trend forces admissions of errors and discovery of lies more quickly, whether by individuals, corporations, or governments. Perhaps more importantly, it requires decisions be made knowing there is a high probability the audit trail will go back to the decision maker.

When these forces add up, in the very near future, we will be faced with a decision we do not face in today's work norms. We will need to be more conscious to use Straight-Line communication because those impactful coworkers around you will be using it. It will be natural to use Straight-Line communication and unnatural to reject it, which is the opposite of what is currently the case. In other words, resisting Straight-Line communication will be like fighting against the adoption of the sewing machine.

Each of these movements I have discussed are technically referred to as **Mega-Trends** by Sociologists. Mega-Trends refer to macro shifts in behavior patterns which impact a whole society. The economists look for Mega-Trends because if they can predict them accurately, it dramatically shifts investment strategies. If you could have predicted the potency of the internet and what it would do to retail purchasing, you would have bought Amazon stock early in its life.

The fact that we face climate change (despite your attribution as to its cause) leads to many investment opportunities if your timing is right.

We have forgotten the outcry at the sewing machine's introduction to outlaw it because it could do the job of fifteen skilled seamstresses and was predicted to create an economic disaster of untold proportions. The fall in costs for clothing, meaning the average working man could (and, more important, would) buy multiple shirts, was not factored into the equation by the doomsday forecasters.

In order to make Straight-Line communication occur, we need a few "shining light" companies where the message is clear. And it will take a few brave innovators/early adopters to visibly take on the mythologies and adopt skills necessary to be effective at making Straight-Line communication the norm.

The result is predictable. We will be faster, more competitive, and better at implementing and making decisions when we give our complete experience, even when it feels vulnerable. When this occurs in a critical mass, the definition of "vulnerable" will change simply because the newly adopted norms will be the expectation and will demand these behavior patterns.

The phrase "regression to the mean" says that circumstances trend to the average; wild deviations (in height, behavior, speed in running, almost anything) are rare. For instance, it is a law that while I may birdie a couple of holes in a round of golf, the probability of my shooting way off my handicap (one way or the other) is pretty small, because I will "regress to my mean score." But the mean is not set in stone. A long layoff, concentrated coaching and practice, or even different clubs, could change my handicap - my mean score in golf.

The mean, or norm, of Straight-Line communication is about to change. Companies not adopting this effective new practice will be the dead buffalo. When we look back, the swiftness of the evolution will feel to some like a revolution.

And finally, there is a case to be made Straight-Line communication will be more easily adopted in an egalitarian society such as America and thus may be one of the major competitive advantages of our nation in the future. It is a fact that our culturally driven autonomy and lack of deference for age leads to a greater propensity for change than in many other cultures. The adoption of these principles in our day-to-day communications may be the next big competitive advantage of our nation, and it may be sustainable for a long time.

The Straight-Line

Appendix

There are way too many works I have drawn on to reference.... however, a listing of the books I have relied on extensively, only some of which I have referred to by title include:

McClelland, D. C. (1995). *Power: The inner experience*. New York, NY: Irvington. (Original   work published in 1975)

Patterson, K., Grenny, J., & Switzler, A. (2002). *Crucial conversations*. New York, NY: McGraw-Hill.

Guterson, D. (1995). *Moneyball*. Stamford, CT: Champion International.

Maister, D. H., Green, C. H., & Galford, R. M. (2002). *The trusted advisor*. London, ENG: Simon & Schuster.

Moore, G. (1991). *Crossing the chasm*. New York, NY: HarperCollins.

Bossidy, L., Charan, R., & Burck, C. (2002). *Execution: The discipline of getting things done*. London, ENG: Random House Business.

Salerno, A., & Brock, L. (2008). *The change cycle*. San Francisco, CA: Berrett-Koehler.

Gladwell, M. (2014*). Tipping point*. New York, NY: Little Brown and Co.

Dweck, C. S. (2006). *Mindset*. London, ENG: Robinson, an imprint of Little, Brown Book Group.

Feynman, R. (1997). *Surely you're joking, mr. feynman*. New York, NY: Robinson, W. W. Norton & Company.

Collins, J. C. (2009). *How the mighty fall: And why some companies never give in.* New York, NY: Collins Business.

Wiersema, F. D. (1995). *The new market leaders: Whos winning and how in the battle for customers.* New York, NY: Free Press.

Pink, D. H. (2009). *Drive.* New York, NY: Riverhead Books.

McClelland, D. C. (2010). *The achieving society.* Mansfield Centre, CT: Martino Publishing. (Original work published in 1961)

Sullivan, G. R., & Harper, M. V. (1996). *Hope is not a method: What business leaders can learn from Americas army.* New York, NY: Broadway Books.

Collins, J. C. (2001). *Good to great: Why some companies make the leap ... and other dont by Jim Collins: Key takeaways, analysis & review.* San Francisco, CA: William Collins.

TZU, S. (2019). *Art of war.* S.l.: WILLIAM COLLINS. (Original work published in 5th Century B.C.)

Bandler, R. (1976). *The structure of magic* (Vol. 1 & 2). Palo Alto, CA: Science and Behavior Books.
Satir, V. (2006). *Peoplemaking.* Barcelona, ES: RBA Integral. (Original work published in 1972)

Bridges, W. (2003). *Managing transitions: Making the most of change.* Boston, MA: Nicholas Brealey.

Gardner, W. L., Avolio, B. J., & Walumbwa, F. (2005). *Authentic leadership theory and practice: Origins, effects and development.* Bingley: Emerald.

Sullivan, G. R., & Harper, M. V. (1997). *Hope is not a method: What business leaders can learn from Americas army.* New York, NY: Broadway Books.

Maister, D. H., Green, C. H., & Galford, R. M. (2002). *The trusted advisor.* London, ENG: Simon & Schuster.

Ware, B. (2012). *The top five regrets of the dying: A life transformed by the dearly departing.* Carlsbad, Calif.: Hay House.

The Straight-Line

About the Author:

Bradford F. Spencer, Ph.D.

Brad is the founder and president of Spencer, Shenk, Capers and Associates (SSCA) located in Los Angeles, California. SSCA is a unique consulting firm specializing in helping businesses grow and their leadership flourish. Their expertise in business strategy compounded by the unusual research-based approach and models has led to the firm's success for over 35 years.

Brad started his career when he was recruited to the Dow Leadership Center associated with Hillsdale College in Michigan following his graduation with a degree in Political Science. This fortuitous position changed the vector of his career and he decided to devote his life to the Applied Behavioral Sciences and helping organizations and people grow their leadership competence. It was here he was first exposed to the potency of many of the concepts in which this book is grounded.

After a brief stop in the corporate training group of Bank of America, he accepted a position with the Training and OD group at Mattel Corp. in Los Angeles. It was here he met Dr. David McClelland of Harvard who has influenced his work and practice heavily.

While at Mattel he was encouraged to expand his business knowledge and was awarded an MBA from Pepperdine University in 1976. Following completion of this program he started studies under Dr. Hedges Capers and in 1984 was awarded his Ph.D. in Clinical Psychology from International College. The combination is unusual and has led the firms focus on leadership stemming from the business imperatives and the daunting personal demons each leader faces. He is noted for his uncanny ability to simplify extremely complex topics, translating them into actions to help his clients meet their goals.

Brad has given numerous addresses, held many board positions and been a member of many professional organizations. His firm has gained a reputation for its impactful research based executive development workshops that have been adopted by numerous corporations as the cornerstone of their high potential development programs.

His wife Connie is a saint and they live in Rolling Hills Estates, Ca. when he is not on an airplane to client's offices around the world. They have one son, Scott, who is testament to the fact that athletic prowess is not genetic and has clearly blown by his father by any metric used. Brad's golfing companions will attest to the fact that he is living proof that memorizing a book on how to play golf does not translate into being a golfer. One day he promises to practice.

About the Author:

Edward L. Monser

Edward L. Monser has served as president of Emerson since 2010. In this role, he drives the company's international growth opportunities and global shared service organizations. He has more than 30 years of experience in senior operational positions at Emerson and has played key roles in globalizing the company. Monser is a member of the company's Office of the Chief Executive and served as Emerson's chief operating officer from 2001-2015.

Monser began his career as a senior engineer at Rosemount in 1981. Rapidly promoted, he was named director of technology in 1987. He went on to hold vice president positions overseeing several critical operations at the Rosemount division before being named president of Emerson's Rosemount business unit in 2001. Under his leadership, Rosemount developed a range of innovative "smart" measurement and analytical devices for the process industry, expanded its service and solutions capabilities, and implemented significant operational efficiencies.

Ed is in great demand because of his expertise in successively promoting international trade. He is a member and a current vice chairman of the U.S.-India Business Council, and he serves on the advisory Economic Development Board for China's Guangdong Province and the board of advisors for South Ural State University in Chelyabinsk, Russia. He also serves on the board of trustees for the international exchange program for mid-career professionals. He is a past board member and past vice chairman of the U.S.-China Business Council.

In the St. Louis community, Monser has served on the boards of directors or trustees for several educational, civic and charitable organizations, including

Ranken Technical College (current chairman) and the Midwest Cargo Hub Commission (vice chairman). In addition, he is a member of the boards of trustees of Illinois Institute of Technology in Chicago and its Armour College of Engineering (chairman). He started his life as a teacher and one of his passions is growing the executive leadership group in Emerson and beyond. Additionally, Monser serves on the board of directors for Air Products and Chemicals, Inc., a company that provides gases and related services for the energy, electronics and manufacturing sectors.

Monser received a bachelor's degree in electrical engineering from Illinois Institute of Technology in 1980. He also has a bachelor's degree in education from Eastern Michigan University and is an alumnus of the executive education program at the Stanford University Graduate School of Business.

Ed has four children of whom he is extremely proud and has recently given birth to a 1968 Corvette Stingray. You will know when he is near you because of the beautiful (and loud) song of the engine.

Made in the USA
Lexington, KY
05 April 2019